Beyond Forgiveness

Patricia Strefling

xulon PRESS

Chapter 1

J anie Cordera's beautiful brown eyes, red-rimmed and hardened with unconcealed loathing, stared at him over the grave of her husband.

"Ashes to ashes and dust to dust…" Reverend Dunham's deep voice echoed as he pronounced the final words over Billy's grave and she had not so much as bowed her head, preferring to yield to her bitterness.

The mid-July wind kicked up whipping her black dress tight against her slender body and Tracson Gage Cordera lowered his eyes, still feeling her dark eyes boring into him. He turned his dusty black Stetson in his work-roughened hands, the silence unbearable. She hated him and he didn't blame her. Trac's sleepless eyes gazed at a Cottonwood leaf as it twirled listlessly and finally landed on Billy's resting place. A moment later the wind lifted the leaf and it was gone, just like Billy.

As soon as Reverend Dunham said *Amen*, Trac spun, punched on his hat and stalked away, his booted heels hitting the ground hard. Walking faster, the memories relentlessly chasing each other in his mind, he snatched the reins of his mount from a low branch and slung himself up into the saddle. Trac Cordera galloped out across the dusty plains without a backward glance. He needed to nurse his pain and try to figure out what to do next.

Trac knew he could not abide for one more minute the suffering that was etched on the anguished faces of those who loved Billy so well. He knew without looking back, that the small group, including Billy's bride of less than a year, was slowly disassembling to go back to their duties. In this wild country, chores had to be done, death or no death.

Finally, after two days of denying his own grief he rode out to Painter's Bluff, Billy's favorite place. Pulling in a deep breath, Trac reined in his mount, slowing him to a walk, jerked off his hat, snapped it on his thigh, dust flying and set it on the saddle horn. His eyes filled as he brushed his fingers through his thick dark brown hair. Looking out over the wide plains, the huge buttes shading him for a moment, he slowly replaced his hat, pulled it down against the sun and let Job, his faithful horse wander at will. Bramble bushes rolled by but Trac was lost, the scenes in his head replaying every detail of the hours they had spent together. Billy whooping and riding right to the edge of the bluff. His eyes roaming the valleys below, determined to find and break the meanest horse in the West for his own mount. Billy's plans for a new Spanish hacienda for his bride. That last desire, the cause for this whole mess.

His cousin and closest friend, was gone. Unable to stop his thoughts, Trac mentally replayed yesterday's agony.

Janie had fallen into his arms, grief overtaking her child-like body. How would he ever forget the feel of her silky brown hair as he'd cupped her head against his chest. Even now the memory of that moment burned a searing guilt stain onto his soul. Trac groaned aloud. He had cherished the moment she'd walked into his arms and hated himself for it. She had been his cousin's wife but Trac had loved her from the first time he'd laid eyes on her.

Chapter 2

Memories kept flooding his mind. The morning after Billy died, before the sun topped the horizon, Trac was at the corral trying to get the black-eyed stallion to stop bucking long enough to release the wild animal back to its natural habitat. He was hoping to save Janie from seeing the horse that killed her husband. He hadn't seen her coming.

She walked up behind him and jerked his arm with more strength than he thought she possessed in her small frame and brought him face to face with her hatred.

"How could you – how could you?" she screamed over and over, emptying her anguish upon his person with flailing fists smashing against his hard chest. Insensible, biting words assaulted his ears; the words even yet burned into his memory. "Why?" She screamed over and over.

He would never forget the look of vengeance etched on her beautiful face. She blamed him for Billy's death. He had stood his ground, bracing his feet wide, arms hanging at his side, letting her beat upon him. After a time, she began to tire and he caught her upper arms only to have her fall against him in defeat.

That one moment had been his undoing. The fact that the fight had gone out of her deepened the dark sorrow that already enslaved his soul. And there was nothing, absolutely nothing he could say or do about it. Billy was dead. Trac knew in this wild land death had no heroes. Billy would not come back and Trac knew he would forever carry the burden of knowing he was guilty of... *what? Not stopping Billy from his willful ways? Billy would've done it anyway*! But Trac *had* involved himself in the bet. For that he would never forgive himself and neither would Janie.

She had jerked out of his embrace and fled sobbing. Trac could only watch her go.

* * *

Why had they made the bet? He wondered, scanning the butte high above his head, the late afternoon sun searing, sweat gathering on his upper lip. Job had sauntered to the flat bed stream for a drink and they stood now together, horse and rider, Trac looking up at the grand mountains, pointed blue peaks in the distance. How could such beauty be before his eyes and yet he not feel it. How many times had he and Billy stood in this very spot, while their horses drank, talking about their dreams, and gazing at the two hundred foot red-brown rock climbing straight up into the blue sky.

He and Billy knew this land, every inch of it, had since they'd come here back in 1865. They had both been nineteen. Dust blew into his burning eyes. He pinched the top of his nose as tears fell slowly down the face of a man who would not only miss his best friend but forever be blamed for his death. *How had it come to this?*

Trac allowed his mount to have his head. Billy had named him Job because it had taken the patience of Job to train the wild beast. Trac smiled at the thought and patted his mount's neck. Billy could train any horse and he'd trained Job well.

There was nothing to do but ride out the pain that bounced around in his rib cage like a stray bullet looking for his heart. It may just as well have pierced it, for all the good it would do now to be alive without Billy. Trac rode for hours, until the stars began to come out of the dark heavens. *Why they were shining at all?*

With little sleep for two days and anguish wringing his heart, he knew one thing. He had to go home. There was his sister Louisa and her children to think about. The homestead. Janie. What would Janie do out at the ranch without Billy? Hardening his heart, he knew he'd spend the rest of his life taking care of her and Billy's ranch, knowing she hated him. Perhaps it was the price he needed to pay. *God knows I can never bring Billy back to you, Janie.*

Trac turned his mount and slowly rode the miles he'd already covered unnoticed. Louisa would be worried and she didn't need any extra concerns right now.

Chapter 3

When Janie knew she was alone, she could finally mourn with the wretched misery that had already overtaken her body and now threatened to consume her soul. As her knees gave way she threw herself across the fresh mound of dirt, the only sign remaining that her precious Billy was there. He lay under the ground only a few feet away but where she could not touch him, could not speak to him, could never again tell him how much she loved him.

Guttural sobs tore from her throat.

"Why God? Why, Billy? I love him. I need him. Why did you take him from me, now? We weren't married a year…not even a year…" Her fingernails gouged into the dirt as though by doing it she could bring herself lower into the grave, nearer her beloved.

Sobs tore from her body until she was hoarse. Then suddenly they stopped. She couldn't remember how or why she'd stopped crying out. Thunder echoed in the distance as the ground rumbled beneath her. Strangely tranquil, she thought it fitting that she should die right here and in her black mourning dress. There was no need for her to live for there was nothing in this world she could want without Billy.

Time passed and hot tears wet the ground beneath her face, causing mud to form on her cheeks. She barely noticed when the rain began to pelt her back and in minutes she was soaked to her skin. Her one desire was that somehow she would sink into the brown earth and die with Billy. That would suit her. Soon her troubled mind felt nothing at all.

* * *

Trac had doubled back and headed for home. The warm rain began to wash over his body. The thunder pounded out the truth, the lightning striking out across the plains in the darkness seemed to verify his own sharp pain. He wished it could wash away the guilt that stained his soul. His heart was as dead as the soaked red-brown earth beneath Job's hooves.

Job headed straight for the barn and Trac noticed he'd left the doors open. Ducking his head they rode into the familiar warmth; he dropped the reins and pulled off the saddle, brushed down his mount with slow movements, filled the feed box with oats, and dropped onto a bed of hay in an empty stall, covering his face with his Stetson. He needed sleep. And comfort from God. God? Where was God? Why hadn't he done something? Why hadn't the storm come two days ago and driven them all inside? Maybe Billy wouldn't be lying up in the little graveyard dead. Sleep would not come and as the storm outside raged around him, the storm within nearly destroyed his soul.

The awful day replayed itself unwanted in his mind, every word seared into his brain as regret wound its savage claws around his heart.

* * *

Billy called out to the ranch hands as he stood at the fence, "Anybody want to place their bets? A gold nugget says I can ride this wild-eyed stallion before the sun is straight up" He laughed swinging his hat in a circle above his head.

Trac had laughed, "You're crazy Billy. That bronc'll send you flying straight over the fence. You're crazier than a three-eyed cat."

But Billy, in his usual manner, proceeded to make it a dare, which he always found pleasure in doing. Billy feared nothing. He had always been the one the girls swooned over and the entire town loved him in spite of his wild and willful ways.

Trac, figuring Billy may have been secretly riding the young stallion and knowing that he probably had a good head on the beast, agreed to the wager. Several of the hands had been lucky enough to possess a few gold nuggets and Billy knew a bet was the surest way to get himself one. In fact Trac had been the one to up the ante. "You ride that black devil and I say we up the stake to two gold nuggets."

The memory of those words bit like a rattlesnake.

Two gold nuggets would be Billy's prize if he could ride the black beast before the sun was straight up. A crowd of men gathered and they went laughing to the corral knowing Billy would win. He mounted the horse with a gleam in his eye. If anyone could tame a stallion Billy could. Trac stood at the fence, slapped his hat against his thigh and settled it down low on his head, waiting to admit his defeat. Truth was, Trac wanted Billy to win. He knew Billy wanted to build a new hacienda for his bride and the gold would go a long way.

The morning sun was already coming across the horizon and it would be a hot one from the looks of it. Billy swung his hat high in the air. He had ridden that black stallion and the sun wasn't even over the butte.

Looking back over his shoulder to antagonize Trac, Billy's whoop of victory ended suddenly when the stallion, wide-eyed and angry, whipped him up and over his head slamming Billy's body to the ground, hard. Trac and the boys ran when he didn't get up. Billy's neck had been broken; his head lay at an odd angle. He could see it as soon as his knees hit the dust. It was over before it had begun and right before their eyes. Trac pulled Billy into his arms as hot bitter tears ran down his dusty face in unbelief.

The men slowly walked away leaving Trac to his grief. After a time, he knew what had to be done. With Billy lying heavy, lifeless in his arms he placed him across Job's neck and hitched himself up into the saddle. He had to take him home to Janie. Heartsick, his gut aching, he turned his mount and slowly treaded across the brush-strewn plains. The Montana winds snatched Billy's hat, tossing it to and fro. Trac watched it bounce over the dusty countryside. Billy would have laughed and chased that hat until he had it back on his head. Trac hadn't the guts to retrieve it. When he rode up to the small cabin Janie had run out laughing. Thinking that Billy was playing one of his silly games, she asked, "Broken ankle Billy?" Trac's heart broke at the look of disbelief as she slowly realized that Billy was not playing. She began to back up, hands over her mouth, her brown eyes searing into his. Her look of absolute horror made him sick to his stomach. Trac dropped down from the saddle and when he pulled Billy's body into his arms, Janie collapsed to the hard ground, screaming the gut-awful sounds he would never forget.

Billy was her life and Trac knew it better than he knew his own heart.

Chapter 4

T rac turned to his side and groaned. Water was running beneath the barn door finally causing him to get up from his bed of grief. He hadn't slept. Gazing toward Louisa's cabin, dusk only a couple of hours away, he trudged up the hill to his sister's house, lifted the latch and let himself in quietly. No sooner had he let the latch fall back in place than he heard the clattering of a carriage as someone drew near. He opened the door quietly and stepped out onto the porch.

"Trac, you've got to come." Came the words from the darkness. He recognized the weak voice instantly. It was Mrs. Preston, Janie's mother.

"She's gone. Janie never came home last night." She called out with a sob.

Trac grabbed his slicker from the peg and shut the door quietly, then whistled. Job appeared after nudging the barn door open and stood in the rain waiting for his master. Trac rode bareback to the barn for his saddle shouting behind him. "Wait here."

Janie's mother waited impatiently while her horse stomped and fretted nervously, the small carriage jerking at each crack of thunder.

Moments later Trac was back, his mount sidestepping, anxious to get to the ride. "Where have you looked?" he shouted through the rainy darkness.

"In the woods, up at her and Billy's cabin." She yelled back. Trac could hear her exhausted words as they echoed through the pounding rain.

"Go home, Mrs. Preston." He yelled over his shoulder. "I know where she is." He took off across the muddy plains.

In the faint light before dawn Trac's eyes searched the shadows of the countryside then reined in his mount. He spotted a small dark hump at the grave site. He should have known she'd never leave Billy. Tired and angry with himself he nudged his mount. Dropping to the ground Trac knelt in the mud. She lay there face down over the grave, her fingers digging into the dirt in grief. Gently he turned her over and sucked in his breath. Her face and body were covered in mud. She lay limp in his arms, her long hair wet and tangled, hung loose down her back. She was soaked through.

His heart thumped with fear. Wiping the mud from her face, he dropped his ear near her mouth. She had breath. With great care he placed his arms beneath her shoulders, then her knees and lifted her slender limp body up to his chest. Rain fell across her face from his Stetson as he looked down, washing some of the mud away, the darkness of her damp eyelashes like a small child's.

Only yesterday he had lain Billy's limp body over his horse for his last ride home. He groaned at the thought he was repeating the scene only with Janie this time. His heart squeezed tightly at the anger he felt in his soul. He would not let her die, too. Not if he had anything to say about it.

Placing her face down across Job's neck, he lifted himself and sat far back on the saddle and then pulled Janie up in front of him. Her muddy arms flopped across his as they made his way slowly but forcefully back to his sister's cabin. Louisa would care for Janie and her place was closer than Mrs. Preston's.

The hideous new daylight was making the way easier, but it sickened Trac to see Janie. She looked dead already, although he knew she was still alive. Hurrying on, for what seemed like hours was only minutes, he kicked at his sister's door and Louisa opened to them immediately.

"I was waiting for you." She whispered. "Come, lay her here, I've prepared a pallet near the fire."

When Trac looked at her questioningly, she explained. "I heard your conversation with Mrs. Preston. Lay her down carefully so we don't wake the children. It will cause an awful hulla-baloo." She tried to ease the tension on her brother's worried face. They'd all been through enough.

Trac dropped to one knee and lay his burden on the pallet.

"Get your wet things off and I'll take care of Janie." She murmured.

Without a word Trac looked into his beloved sister's eyes. She soothed him with gentle words while she removed Janie's heavy outer clothing.

"Hand me the blanket from the rocker." She whispered, leaning closer to Janie to feel her breath. "She's alive. Grief has overtaken her but I am worried she will be ill with consumption if we don't get her out of these wet clothes and into a dry gown."

Trac's face gave nothing away as he retrieved the blanket with quick, sharp intensity. "I'll put water on to heat."

Louisa could hear the frustration in her brother's voice. "That will help. I'll get her cleaned up." She said quietly as she tossed the blanket over a taut length of rope she'd prepared earlier, cre-ating a makeshift room.

Trac turned his back and busied himself at the stove, setting water on to heat, trying not to make noise that might wake the little ones. Emmett, Louisa's husband had been gone nearly six months now searching for gold. Trac wondered how he could leave his wife and two little girls for so long, but he knew Emmett was a smart man and wanted more than anything to make a good life for Louisa. He wished Emmett were here.

Trac heard Janie's quiet groan and started to go to her. Realizing he was still dripping wet, he pulled off his slicker and duster, and hung them over a nail near the door. He yanked off his shirt and hung it over a chair and set it near the fire. The rest of his soaked clothes would have to wait.

Pacing the small area between the blanket and table he let his mind wander back to his younger days. He and Billy, sons of brothers, were born only two months apart, Billy the elder of the two. Trac, a full four inches taller than Billy, possessed only half of his cousin's charisma, and was practical and patient to a fault. Billy loved and respected horses, women, and his grandfather's whittling knife. He could whittle out a lifelike bird from a large stick in a couple of hours, not to mention the fact that he was more fun to be around than any other man Trac knew. Billy's dark good looks and sincere love of everything and everyone he met was distinguishable in the fact that he was consistently happy, no matter what befell him.

"Trac, stop pacing, you'll wake the children." Louisa whispered behind the curtain.

He pulled out a chair and sat at the table, head in his hands, too tired to sleep and too tired to forget. His mind went right on remembering.

Trac knew Billy had lived his new life in carefree abandon and knew no enemy except maybe a young Josiah Wilson for stealing his girl – Janie. Josiah, at age nine, had declared his love for the brown-haired, brown-eyed Janie Preston, telling everyone he would marry her some day. Janie had barely noticed Josiah, but everyone in Stonewall knew he intended to marry her any way he could – until Billy Cordera came into town. Trac smiled. He remembered the day clearly.

He and Billy had just come from Texas after their first cattle run, more than fifteen hundred head, longhorns mostly. They were young and bullheaded and proud, had new duds, and were celebrating their recent success in Stonewall. Only nineteen at the time, they were men of the world, each possessing more money than they'd ever had. They had chosen Stonewall to settle in and had come to town to spend some of their cash and bank the rest.

Janie and her sister Elizabeth had just come out of Logan's Millinery Shoppe and nearly ran headlong into the two of them. Billy, always the gentleman, had smiled in his easy-going manner and lifted his brand new black Stetson off his dark head, "Excuse us, ladies, for our clumsiness." He had sidestepped with a slight bow and his handsome smile, to let them pass.

Elizabeth, taller, light-haired and green-eyed had sniffed at him properly, stuck her chin in the air and held her full skirts out and away as she passed the two fresh young cowboys. Janie, younger, smaller and dark-eyed, stood staring at Billy shyly. Seeing her sister had not followed, Elizabeth looked over her shoulder, "Janie, come this instant. It isn't polite to stare." She huffed and grabbed her sister's elbow.

Billy made a funny face at the proper Elizabeth's back, noting Janie had wriggled out of her sister's embrace. The young dark-haired Janie had laughed quietly at Billy's antics then had run after her sister, her cheeks flushed. Trac thought Janie the prettiest girl he'd ever laid eyes on and noticed immediately she had acknowledged him only so much as to be polite but had not looked in his eyes the way she had looked into Billy's.

"Billy, that little gal sure had eyes for you." Trac had teased quietly.

"Nah, she's too young for me." Billy had thrown back over his shoulder. "But that sister of hers sure wears her boots high, don't she?" He laughed. "You'd think she owned the whole town or somethin'. And here we are in our best duds." He shrugged and went on, anxious to spend some of the money hiding deep in a pocket of his brand new pair of trousers.

Trac remembered Billy never took anyone or anything seriously, whereas he himself was more staid, solid, serious. That's the way it had always been – Billy the teaser, Trac the tamer. Now Billy was gone. How could God have taken him first? He, with Janie and all? *It should have been me instead.*

Another moan from behind the blanket set him to pacing again. Why didn't Louisa say something? He turned and found himself looking into the eyes of a very tiny little girl, the image of his sister. "Virginia" he crouched his six foot two frame down to her eye level. She smiled shyly looking around him.

"Where's Ma?"

"She's behind that curtain taking care of Miss Janie, honey. She'll be out in a minute or two. Want Uncle Trac to get you a drink?"

"No. Can I go outside? I want to see if mama's flowers are wet."

Standing to his full height, he smiled slightly as she lifted her white nightgown from around her little-girl feet and scurried to the door, looking up for him to open it. Trac stepped out with her and saw that the sun was creeping up higher now after the all-night rain.

He waited for her to see the flowers for herself and hustled her back inside. "Mama?" she called.

"Honey, Mama is helping Miss Janie. I'll be out in a minute. You sit at the table with Uncle Trac and wait won't you?"

"Yes, Mama." Four-year-old Virginia replied and climbed up on the bench, sticking her elbows on the table and her chin in her small hands.

"Good girl." Trac teased his niece as she tried to hide her smile behind her hands. He reached out and pushed the strands of dark hair out of her eyes thinking how she looked so much like their own mother. Just then four-month-old Grace made her presence known by crying out.

"Mama, Grace wants to nurse."

"Thank you, Virginia." Louisa called back, then came round the curtain. "Trac, Janie's dry and sleeping now. Perhaps you should go tell her mother she's safe." She reached up and patted his broad shoulders gazing for a moment into his black-brown eyes, then moved to attend to Grace.

"Will she be all right?" Trac called after her.

"Janie'll be fine. You go on now. Her mother's no doubt worried sick."

Trac set Virginia in a chair with a piece of bread, the butter crock nearby, grabbed his half-dry shirt and pulled on his still-soaked duster. Stepping outside, he whistled and Job came.

* * *

"Sara, Janie's at Louisa's and she's resting."

Janie's mother was overwrought with worry but happy to know her daughter was alive. After all the small family had been through, another death would be devastating. There was already too much of that, what with the gold rush and all. People brought diseases, they shot each other over the smallest nugget of gold, and the entire territory was at unrest with the Cheyenne Indian nation. It was all they could do to raise and sell their cattle while trying to live on this harsh but beautiful land. Besides the hard work and long hours, a frigid, unforgiving Montana winter would be upon them soon enough. Then all the gold diggers would be looking for a place to settle in for the cold months.

"Where in the name of Providence was she, Trac?" He realized Mrs. Preston was speaking, her voice weak, her hands fluttering above her heart.

"At the grave." His voice was hoarse from lack of sleep.

"Oh my." Her hands flew to her cheeks. "I should have known. I checked the cabin first thinking she had gone home and then I checked out by the stand of cottonwoods where she and Billy used to go. I didn't think to look . . . "

"She should be all right now." He interrupted knowing the words weren't true. Janie, without Billy, would never be all right. "Louisa's good at nursing and she says what Janie needs is rest."

"Of course she's in good hands. Thank you for bringing her home, Trac." She reached up to pat his shoulder and sighed, "I must get my chores done so I can visit my daughter."

"Stay inside and bake me a pie, Mrs. Preston, and I'll get your chores done. She'll be sleeping for awhile." Trac said quietly and quit the cabin before she could interfere with his plans. He needed to work.

Billy's men had already fed and watered the cattle. Slopping through the mud-soaked grounds, he mended two fence posts and mucked out the barn. Work kept his mind busy for the next few hours. Tired and needing sleep, he returned to the older woman's table.

"Thanks for the pie, Mrs. Preston. Best when it's warm. I'll be going now." He lifted his hat off the nail and started for the door needing to be alone. "I'll be back in a few days, see how things are going."

"Trac."

"Yes, ma'am."

"It wasn't your fault."

Trac said nothing, pulled his hat tight on his head, nodded politely, and left the cabin without a word. He'd been awake for almost two days, ever since Billy died. Right now he needed hard work and then tonight perhaps he could sleep. Job came and he settled into his worn saddle, comforted by the warmth at his knees, glad for his faithful animal. He rode toward home.

Chapter 5

Trac stared out over the lay of the land. Helena, the gold-mining town was a good hundred miles west. His and Billy's fathers had bought this land long before the gold rush in 1839. The two young Cordera brothers, Roberto and Miguel had come from eastern Texas as ranch hands looking for a place of their own. They'd stopped in Helena and gone further west to settle a big parcel of land where they could raise cattle. They had loved the mountains, the buttes, and the plains of Idaho Territory later to become Montana. Youngest of the four brothers, they wanted to strike out on their own and left the two elder brothers to work the Texas ranch with their father.

Their mother had died ten years before when diphtheria nearly wiped out the entire town. And when they returned to Texas they found their father had passed on leaving his four sons their full inheritance.

Roberto and Miguel, already nearing thirty and thirty-two made a pact to return. One year later they drove their herd across the mountains and arrived in late September and claimed 180 acres apiece and built a small cabin near the property line, finished a large enough fenced in place to hold their cattle and made it through their first bitter cold Montana winter.

The Cordera brothers, their mother a Spanish beauty, had inherited her black eyes and hair and her hard-working ways. They had upset the entire female population, est. 257 including children, of Stonewall. The town was known for it's quiet living. Most folks had fled the too-busy city of Helena to build at Stonewall which was situated on the valley floor in between two large buttes. Being of good looks and well-to-do-means, the brothers had chosen two sisters to marry after living as bachelors for over two years.

During that time they built themselves a home apiece, brought more cattle up from Texas, and began their ranching days. The double wedding of the Cordera brothers was talked about for years afterward. It was said no other wedding had been more splendid. The courting had taken nearly two years to complete and the town had watched with bated breath as to whether the boys would marry the same day or choose separate days. When the news had finally been announced and the gold wedding bands had arrived all the way from Boston, it had been a grand day.

The Barnard girls, one fair, one dark, were beautiful, talented and rich. Their father, the good Mr. Oliver Barnard, town banker, and his lovely wife Delia, the richest family in Stonewall, had invited the entire town to the stately affair. The dresses were said to have come from a Paris designer, but no one really knew for sure. Fortunately there was a large church in the small town, built by the Barnards, and it provided the appropriate background for such fine weddings, which included organ music and the magnificent French wine brought in by rail.

Portraits of the entire wedding party which some said numbered upward of twenty, had been painted by a New York artist brought in especially for the event and even the large carriage owned by the Barnards drove through the city in all its grandeur, decorated with white satin bows, so all could see the beautiful brides and their handsome new husbands. It was said that Mrs. Barnard put her foot down when it came to hanging cow bells on the carriage.

The Cordera ranch had become two homesteads now that the brothers each had a wife. The properties, sitting side by side, encompassed an entire region covering nearly 400 acres. The Cordera children that followed had been raised on acres of flat-lands and had ridden the mile and miles of countryside to their heart's content.

Billy had been the only child of the elder brother, Roberto; Trac was the first-born of the younger brother Miguel, three sisters arriving after him. First-born sons only two months apart, Billy and Trac had been forever joined together, as cousins and best friends.

Now everything had changed. Death had claimed both fathers and Trac's mother. Billy's mother had given her son and his new wife the ranch less than a year ago at their wedding and had gone back east to live out the rest of her years. She was too elderly to make the trip back so soon and Trac knew she would be alone in her grief.

His own thoughts caused him to become more bitter in spite of the fact his mother had always taught him to trust God. She had been a Sunday school teacher in her uncle's church. He missed her terribly and wished that for just a moment he could look into her soft brown eyes and have her tell him everything would be all right.

Chapter 6

Revolting thoughts escaped Trac's mind and made their way into his heart. He should have stopped Billy . . . not assumed he'd ridden the stallion before that day and cautioned him. Instead he had upped the ante. That was the reason Billy went to all the trouble. Billy wanted to build Janie a beautiful Spanish hacienda. Because of Trac's foolishness he left Janie a widow after only ten months of marriage.

It was his place to look out for Janie, now. But he couldn't do it. He had feelings for Janie, always had. He'd never allowed himself to show even a hint of those feelings and had always kept them to himself. She hated him now and he was glad. Maybe that would make things easier, if by God's grace, they ever could be right again.

The bitterness he held in his heart for his part in Billy's death would never leave. He knew it now. There was nothing else to do but go back. His sisters needed him. Janie would marry another and that would be the end of it. Determination settled into his heart like a cold stone. He turned and headed back to his ranch. There was work to be done.

"Louisa." He called out as he entered the ranch house at dusk.

"In here, Trac. Shhh. . . the girls are asleep, finally. Janie's still asleep, too. She's exhausted."

He threw his hat on the nail by the door and pulled out a chair. "She's going to be all right then?" He asked quietly, avoiding Louisa's eyes as he reached for a cup and poured from the tin pot on the stove.

"Yes – her heart is broken, but she'll heal. She just needs time."

Trac was silent as he watched his sister move about the large room, glad she could live in the family ranch home. When their father died, Trac moved down to the bunkhouse with the ranch hands and took a bed there so Emmett, Louisa and their babies could have the house. The eldest sister, Margaret, had married well and moved east some five years past. Margaret had invited Molly, their youngest sister, to stay for the summer. Molly was the image of his mother as was Louisa and was of great company to Louisa with her two little ones to care for while Emmett was searching for his fortune in gold.

Louisa set a plate of beans and pork on the oblong wooden table, along with buttered biscuits. She set a tin of cooled milk alongside his plate and laid her hand on his shoulder.

"Trac, you have to eat. You need to stay strong for us...for all of us." Louisa was going to cry and he didn't know if he could abide that, so he picked up his spoon and ate. Louisa slipped away and he found himself eating alone.

A few minutes later, she returned from the bedroom, eyes red but her small mouth set. She picked up his dishes and said in a shaky voice, "Trac, it wasn't your fault. You know how Billy was. He paid no mind to any of us and did as he pleased. You know that." She whispered now, looking over her shoulder, hoping Janie was still asleep, then continued.

"Providence doesn't always make things easier, but harder. We have to bear it. Janie will learn to bear it, too, in time." She continued with a look of pleading in her brown eyes.

Trac looked up and Louisa saw the agony in his face, just as she saw him cover it up and stand to his feet.

"Providence allows for us to make our own choices, too, Louisa." He stated firmly and upon settling his hat turned on his booted heel and walked out the door, glancing once at the corner where Janie lay.

"Oh Trac." Louisa whispered as the door closed behind her brother's strong back.

Chapter 7

Trac headed for the bunkhouse where his men would be coming in for supper. His cook, Weston Clancy was just spooning up the soup. "Wes, I've eaten. I'll be in my office catching up on paperwork. Don't disturb me tonight."

"Yep, sure boss. Gotcha." He waved his hand but the door had already slammed. Hard.

Trac was determined to pick up where he'd left off for the sake of his men. He had a ranch to run and several of them were married and needed their paychecks. Besides where could he go and not be reminded of Billy...and Janie?

Hours later, he emerged into the darkness of the bunkhouse, his head aching. He slipped out into the night, careful not to disturb the sleeping men, their snores loud enough to wake the dead. Too soon they'd be in their saddles again for a week's worth of gathering strays and they needed a good night's rest.

A walk in the light of the moon's bright face reminded him that Billy's soul was so far away and all because he'd been careless. Hardening his heart he returned to his bunk, tossed off his trousers and fell into his bed and tried to sleep.

After a few hours of hard sleep then an hour of tossing around he rose an hour before dawn and stood at the back bunkhouse door gazing up at the ranch house. A tiny single light shone in one corner window. Probably Louisa feeding the baby.

Sometime later, he quietly packed up a saddle bag, grabbed a couple of biscuits and gulped a cup of scalding coffee, which always boiled on the old wood stove, and headed out to the barn.

Patting his mount's neck, he knew Job sensed his grief and nudged him. "Hey, boy, you're missing Billy, too aren't you?"

Running his fingers through his hair, he put on his Stetson, grabbed his gloves and headed out for a day's work on the range. Riding up past the ranch house he thought he saw a figure in the quiet darkness, standing at the railing on the wraparound porch. He looked again and it was gone. Janie?

What if it was? He had no right to know. No right at all. He found himself galloping away at breakneck speed as though he could outrun his own heart.

With Janie safely at his sister's he hoped to repair the fences on her property. Billy's men had their hands full with the chores. Heavy-hearted, he rode along the entire perimeter inspecting every corner. If anything was awry, he jumped down, fixed what he could and got back in the saddle again. The task took hours, but now he knew where the weaknesses in the fences were and tomorrow he'd come back and repair every last one of them.

Riding Billy's ranch fueled his frustration. Everywhere he looked Billy was there. Laughing in the fields as children, swimming in the wide-bed stream, standing in the shade of the cottonwoods with their hats swishing at bugs in the summertime, kicking up dirt, Billy kissing Janie goodbye up at the ranch house. It hurt like crazy every time he remembered anything. Was anything so desolate and lonely as loving someone one minute and knowing the next you'd never see them again?

God, I can't even pray.

Driven by the need to work, Trac spent the next several days alone working at Billy's ranch in the daytime, eating supper with Louisa and the girls, then down to the bunkhouse for paperwork and sleep. Thankfully Janie had gone to her mother's. He could breathe easier.

His men were gathering up strays, they'd be camping for at least two weeks, riding the ranges.

Picking up the lantern, he set it next to the bath and glad for the quiet, eased into the warm water and washed the dust from his tired body, wishing he could wash the stain from his soul. As he lifted himself from the water, it sluiced down his sun-darkened body. Grabbing the towel, he wrapped it around his middle and sat on the bunk. There on the small wood table lay his mother's Bible. Worn and torn, he picked it up. The weight of it seemed too heavy and he laid it back down. *Lord, I know you're there.*

The winds kicked up outdoors and he walked to the tiny window in his office to look out. Bramble bushes were blowing like the tumbleweeds they were named for. Not a good sign. If the heat and winds picked up, dust storms would hinder the men's work. Driven by that thought, he pulled off the wet towel, tossed it at his desk chair, and climbed into bed, pulling the covers up and over his head. *What I need is a good night's sleep.*

At dawn the next morning he woke to a vicious dust storm. It blew and whipped around the corners and whistled in the ceilings. Storm or no storm he had to feed the cattle and finish Billy's work. Pulling on his heavy Levis and chaps, then a dark, heavy workshirt, he grabbed his boots and fit them on.

Wes, the bunkhouse cook, was gone with the men so he helped himself to a slice of beef, a couple of biscuits and coffee, then packed a few extra biscuits for later. It was too early to disturb Louisa and the girls. When he opened the door, the wind caught it from his gloved hands and sent it flying back against the bunkhouse wall, nearly sweeping his Stetson away....*like Billy's. Why did everything that happened have to remind him of Billy?*

Muscling the door shut, he tied a bandana around his mouth and nose, held on to his hat and walked against the powerful wind to the barn where Job greeted him. "Best we put some shades around your eyes, buddy, else you'll not likely enjoy today's weather." He patted his mount and saddled him up, remembering to pack the necessary tools in a leather bag.

It took all of his strength to open the barn door against the wind. "Whoa, Job. 'Atta boy."

Job sidestepped whipping his head away from the wind so his nostrils would not take in air. Trac leaned into the wind holding onto his hat, wishing he'd thought to bring the leather strings to tie it under his chin. It'd be a fight all day to keep his hat if the wind kept up.

"Easy boy. Easy. C'mon let's ride with our backsides to the wind, let you catch your breath." He turned his mount's head and started for Billy's ranch. After a time, the wind played itself out and as the sun came out bright, white clouds moved lazily through the blue skies.

Pulling his hat off and wiping his face with his kerchief, Trac observed the work he just finished. Fences were repaired around the perimeter. That had taken the entire day. Hungry, he sat down under a tree for shade and heard the sound. Hissing. Careful not to move too fast, he let his eyes roam toward the sound, slowly reaching for his pistol. Ten seconds later the biggest rattler he'd laid eyes on lay dead not ten feet away.

He picked up the huge snake and tossed it in the field, food for the birds. Above all things he hated rattlers. Unsettled, he looked around to make sure there weren't more and ate.

Trac worked for more than a week at Billy's place and was finally satisfied. Cattle were fenced and fed. Billy's men had rounded up the strays, but Trac knew they wouldn't stay at the ranch if they had to take orders from a woman and Janie was not up to the task. Trac met with the men, listened to their concerns and appointed the best man foreman.

Janie would have to do the watering and feeding because most of Billy's men were married men who went home to their families for the winter. In the back of his mind he knew he didn't want any single men or drifters hanging around to take advantage of Janie. She was too vulnerable, not to mention the fact she now owned one of the largest ranches in Stonewall.

He hoped she would abide him long enough for him to show her how to feed and water them until Spring when her crew returned.

Suddenly Trac felt the weight of all that was left to him. Sure, Billy had a little money set back, but he'd been a big spender. Sailing Janie off to Europe for their honeymoon had taken a huge chunk out of Billy's savings. There wasn't that much cash left. Thus the bet that day. Billy had another dream: to build his beautiful new wife a hacienda the style of which was like his Spanish grandmother's...the one his grandfather had built for his wife.

Beautiful and costly. Trac knew Billy's every dream for the future. Sick, he tried not to think about it. *Billy, I'd give my life to have you back here with Janie.*

Chapter 8

"**B**oss you're workin' too long and too late." Wes chastised him one evening two weeks later. "You'll die an easy death, you keep that up." He wagged his finger as he set the still-warm plate of food on Trac's desk. "Killing yourself ain't gonna bring Billy back."

Trac looked up from his work. "Don't worry Wes, work never hurt anybody." Trac picked up his spoon and dug in without another word.

"Yep, only kills 'em if'n they don't bother to rest none. Even God rested." Trac looked up in time to see his cook disappear through the low doorway.

"Mind your own business." Wes heard as he walked to the kitchen and mumbled under his breath, "I am."

Sleep came easier these days, Trac noticed. He had not set eyes on Janie since the day he brought her to Louisa's from Billy's grave.

"You talked to Janie?" Wes was back at his door.

"Nope, don't plan to."

Wes noted Trac's dark eyes, red rimmed, and annoyed at the interruption. "Seems ta me, 'course I ain't sayin' I'm the smartest bunkhouse hand you got 'round here, that you'd be wantin' to clear things up an all."

"Clear what up, Wes? That I'm the reason Billy's dead?"

"Aw, you ain't believin' that are ya? Everybody round here knows . . .

Trac cut him off. "Look Wes, everyone around here knows if I hadn't made that bet, Billy'd be here today...with Janie."

"Well, guess you'd be the only one believin' that." He said smartly.

Trac watched the short, bow-legged old cowboy walk away.

"Janie'll tell ya the truth..." Trac mumbled under his breath, sick to death of his own nagging fault-finding.

Throwing the pencil on the desk, he kicked up his booted feet and rested them on the desktop, setting his chair back on two legs, allowed himself time to straighten his aching back. "Can't get anything done around here without somebody buttin' in." He muttered to no one.

Perhaps Janie would go back east with Billy's mother. Then he could breathe again. She could marry up with some gentleman and forget about Montana and ranching.

The August sun was going down quickly. It was the first of the month and payments were due at the bank tomorrow. Rising from his chair, he slammed a rock down on his papers, left the window cracked for air, and stalked out of the bunkhouse.

Trac saddled Job and turned his mount west and rode into the sunset, watching the blues, pinks and oranges transform the evening sky, moment by moment, over the craggy mountaintops. He'd never tire of the variation at each evening's sunset. Letting Job lead, he rested in the familiar seat of his saddle, and glad for the late evening quiet, moseyed along for a good while, then headed over to check Janie's place. There was movement in the shadows. A feminine figure. As he approached slowly, still hidden from view, he saw that it was Janie.

He turned Job immediately and meandered in the opposite direction hoping she had not seen him. Why wasn't Janie's mother keeping a better eye on her? Barely a month had passed and Janie was home alone? Trac didn't want her there.

He knew he had to face her sometime, but now was not the time. The last time Janie had looked at him was over Billy's grave. That had been the last he ever hoped to see that look again. Her accusing eyes and broken heart served his memory well by reminding him constantly of his failure to save Billy's life. If he hadn't been so quick to make that wager.

Well, there's no hope for it now, the deed is done and over with. You'd best be getting back home and minding your own business.

The next morning Wes was shaking him awake. "Boss, Louisa's lookin' for ya. Says it's important."

"Louisa?" Trac lifted himself out of a dead sleep and smoothed his long, scraggly dark hair away from his unshaven face. He grabbed his trousers and pulled them on, then tugged the suspenders over his shoulders and snagged a shirt, pulling it on as he walked to the front of the bunkhouse.

As soon as he saw her face and her arms crossed over her chest, he knew there was trouble . . . "Trac..." she whispered, taking his arm and towing him into a private corner. "She's left her mothers and gone back home."

"Who?" Trac rubbed his whiskered chin, still half asleep.

"Janie...she's gone back home."

"Is she doing better then?"

"She acts like she is, but I know she isn't ready to run the ranch." Louisa's hands were on her hips. That was a bad sign.

"What am I supposed to do, Louisa?" Trac ran his fingers through his hair, not bothering to mention the fact that he'd seen Janie and totally agreed with his sister.

"Trac, for pity's sake, the girl has just lost her husband and she can't take on the chores of a 200-acre ranch. She'll kill herself. You *have* to talk to her."

Trac stared at his sister, small but determined. "What could I possibly say to her, Louisa?"

"You just march over there and tell her how sorry you are about everything and that she's to go back to her mother."

"What? I'll do no such thing. She has a mind of her own. I've finished mending the fences and Billy's men will tend to the chores until the first snow flies. Besides, nothing I say will be welcome. You oughta know that, Lou."

"Look, Trac, you have to face her sometime." His sister said smartly, then turned and marched back up the hill, her back stiff as the trunk of an ancient oak.

Trac knew she was right, but he mumbled under his breath. *"Not yet I don't."*

Unable to go back to sleep, he washed up, ate breakfast, and talked to several of his trusted hands about the work that needed to be done today, then decided he'd ride with two of them to look for strays.

He hadn't planned on spending the day out on the range; but had less desire to speak with Janie just yet.

"We'll be late tonight, so leave our plates in the warming oven, Wes."

"Yep, sure will, boss."

They rode out and when Trac looked back he saw Louisa standing at the front door with her hands on her hips, her dark hair whipping in the wind.

Chapter 9

Janie tied on her apron and set to work in her own kitchen, now dusty with the latest wind storm. She'd cried long enough. Her heart had been broken in two and Billy was gone. There was nothing she could do about it except one thing. She could hate Trac Cordera.

That one thing kept her going. Her bitterness toward him grew every day. She was surrounded with the Cordera family . . . everyone except Billy. She was alone except for her own mother, whom she loved dearly. But she and her mother were two different people and rarely saw eye to eye on any subject.

One thing she knew for certain, she would not let her love for Billy die. Not now. Not ever.

"Blue, come here you old mangy thing." Janie leaned down to pet the old sheepdog, long retired from service. "You miss your master don't you?" Tears came to her eyes and she started to crumble. "I miss him, too."

By the time she rose from the rocking chair it was dark. Hours had passed while she sat whiling them away. Making her way to the bed, she was suddenly afraid of being alone in the dark. She'd never lived alone before. She'd gone from her father's house to Billy's. Her father had died only 3 days after Billy had asked for her hand and given his betrothal promise. *Daddy I miss you so much. You would have known what to do.*

Her hands shaking, she reached for the match box which fell to the wooden floor, matches skittering in every direction like stars falling from heaven. She crumpled to a heap in frustration, hot bitter tears burning down her cheeks.

I love you Billy. No one loved you the way I did. How could you leave me? She cried to a dark and quiet house, knowing her loneliness had only begun. After a long while she rose shakily to her feet and stumbled into their bedroom where they had sealed their wedding vows with their love. Throwing herself upon the quilted bed, she grabbed Billy's blue denim shirt, his favorite, and clung to it sobbing, the slight fragrance of his skin still there when he wasn't and never would be again. It was hours before her tired mind would let her go to sleep. But before she did she whispered, "I hate you, Tracson Cordera. I'll hate you for the rest of my life."

Morning came but Janie had no desire to raise herself from the bed. The rain falling on the roof overhead reminded her of the day Billy's precious body was laid in the ground. She didn't remember how she'd gotten to Louisa's and was glad, for Louisa said quietly that Trac had found her and brought her home. Her skin crawled to think he had touched her. It was because of him that she was a widow.

The rain continued, while a sense of tranquility and repose embraced her. She felt nothing. For hours she lay there trying to sleep, to calm her raging mind, free it of thoughts of Billy, of her loneliness. Unable to do so, she arose and walked to the outhouse in her rumpled clothes. As she exited the tiny door she saw Louisa and her two little ones coming over the hill. She hadn't even noticed the rain had stopped.

"Oh no." she cried then calmed herself. Why hide? Why pretend she was alive anyway....why should she hide herself and pretend she was all right when she wasn't?

"Janie, you're up. It's so good to see . . ." Louisa stopped midsentence as she laid eyes on Janie. "Didn't you sleep last night?" she asked gently, gathering her skirts, holding them against the strong winds.

"Of course, Louisa. I just didn't bother to undress." She said irritably and continued her hard-heeled trek to the cabin.

Louisa sighed as she followed. "I've brought the girls to visit." She stated unnecessarily and noticed the matches laying asunder on the floor. "Virginia, dear, pick up Janie's matches. They must have fallen." She spoke kindly, smiling down at her eldest.

"Okay, Mama."

"That's a dear. Now Grace and I shall sit in the rocker until she's asleep and then we will help Janie."

"I don't need any help, Louisa." Janie stated flatly. "I prefer to do my own housework. In fact, I'm staying here for good."

"Oh Janie, you can't stay here." Louisa said in disbelief. "Billy wouldn't have wanted that."

"You don't know what Billy would have wanted. I do." Her voice sounded so bitter that Louisa looked at her with pity in her eyes. This irritated Janie all the more.

"I can't abide the way you look at me, Louisa." She stomped from the room, then called out over her shoulder, "Why don't you go home?"

Louisa heard the bedroom door slam hard enough to rattle the dishes on the wall.

"Mama, why is Janie so angry?"

"Virginia, sometimes people that are hurt inside act hurt outside, too. Don't fret, dear. Things will calm down when Janie gets better. For now, let's clean up."

Louisa rose from her chair carefully and laid a sleeping Grace on a pallet underneath the window where she would get a breeze, then proceeded to sweep the puncheon floor until it was neat and clean.

"Virginia, while I'm working why don't you snap the ends off this batch of beans and we'll set them to cooking." Virginia obeyed, while Louisa carried a large pot of boiling water to the hearth.

"Janie, where is your lye soap?"

"It's underneath the basin," Janie called back tiredly, then, "Louisa, what are you doing?"

"We're going to wash. It's Monday."

"I haven't worn hardly anything. And I don't feel like washing. Just leave me be."

Ignoring Janie's tired voice, Louisa set herself to singing quietly. When she entered the small bedroom and tiptoed quietly gathering up Billy's clothes, Janie launched into an impossible fit. "Don't touch Billy's things. I want them left where they are!" she screamed. "Don't move them!" Before she knew what was happening Louisa found herself being pushed from the room, the door slamming against her face. The bolt slid across angrily.

"Come Virginia, let's gather up Grace and go home. Janie needs to be alone."

Virginia came to her, but there were tears in the little brown eyes. "There dear. It's all right. Janie doesn't mean anything bad. She's just hurt. She'll be better, okay?"

"Okay, mama." Virginia cried, wiping her eyes.

Louisa hugged her eldest daughter, then picked up Grace. She and the girls walked through the pastures, knowing that when winter came the walking would cease. She wished Emmett would come home. Tears fell from her face when she let her mind wander too far from her faith as she thought about what she would do if Emmett died, like Billy had.

Inside Janie heard the quietness of the house and felt a blanket of guilt cover her. Louisa was only trying to help . . . her conscience argued. Janie threw herself across the bed and clutched Billy's clothing to her chest. "My handsome, funny, Billy." She whispered. "Why did you leave me?"

An hour later, after several stops to pick late blooming wildflowers, Louisa put Grace on a pallet nearby and set Virginia to work writing her numbers and letters, then pulled her Bible from the bookcase Emmett had so lovingly built for her, and sat in the rocker. She needed comfort from the pain that clung to her heart. Janie's sorrow hurt her deeply and there was nothing she could do to make it better. Her fingers fell onto the pages and she found 1 Peter 5:7 where the petals from a long-dried once-yellow flower lay snuggled. "Casting all your care upon him; for he careth for you." She read aloud.

"Lord." Louisa prayed, "I cannot do anything without your help. Be with Janie. She misses Billy so. Please be with Emmett, too. And Molly as she returns home to us in the spring. And help me to love Janie."

Grace cried out for her mother and Louisa reached down to pick up her chubby red-haired child to nurse.

"Virginia, please put your dolly and her little cottage away. We want to have a tidy house." *In case your father comes home.* She wanted to add, but dared not.

"Yes, Mama, but dolly has to sleep in it at night."

"Of course, dear." Virginia loved her dolly. Molly had sewn the doll from some old scraps before she'd gone East to visit Margaret. Trac had made the cottage house and Billy had whittled two miniature birds to set upon the thatched roof.

The wind began to pick up. It was already the third week of August and Emmett would surely come before the snow closed the passes. Louisa wanted the house clean from floor to rooftop. A full house was what Louisa loved best . . . but if Emmett did not come this winter, it would be a long one. And that meant Grace would be nearly a year old before her father saw her again. And Virginia would have passed her fifth year.

"Virginia, sit with the baby on the quilt while I get the clothes off the line. The wind has picked up." Louisa's dress whipped against her legs with gusting force. Suddenly her eye caught sight of a snippet of cloth as it blew and tumbled over the ground. She ran after her undergarments finally laying hands upon the elusive material and laughed as she snatched the dry clothing from the makeshift line. Emmett had stretched a precious piece of rope between two tall trees right next to the house.

"Any longer and we'd have our unmentionables flying all of the Territory of Montana and who knows who might find them blowing about." She teased her daughter, smoothing her hair as she passed. Serious Virginia giggled heartily.

"Oh Mama." Virginia responded. "You are funny."

"Only because I love my little girls so." Louisa patted her daughter's dark head so much like her own, and rinsed the second batch of clothing, humming as she went. The afternoon passed quickly. All their things had dried quickly, thanks to the gusty winds, folded and put away.

Trac knocked twice and entered the ranch house.

"Come in Trac. Supper's almost ready and I need to talk with you about Molly."

Trac aimed his hat for the nail snagging it easily from a four foot distance, then washed the dust from his face and hands over the washing bowl. Growling loudly he reached down to pick up Virginia and give her a twirl.

"Stop Uncle Trac, you're making me silly-minded."

Trac let her down gently and looked in the cradle at the sleeping Grace.

"Grace sure looks like her pa."

"She does, doesn't she? All that red hair." Louisa sighed, "I miss him so much."

Trac stopped to look at his sister. "You doing okay, sis?"

"Of course, just miss my husband, that's all." She changed her facial expression quickly knowing her brother had enough on his mind without worrying about her.

"Sit yourself down. I've got your favorite supper, fried chicken and red potatoes with snap beans. And we need to talk." Louisa sat the bowls of hot food on the table.

Trac sat down and pulled out a chair for Virginia, who sat and immediately bowed her head to pray. Louisa nodded for her to go ahead.

"Jesus thank you for this food and for Mommy, Daddy, Grace and Uncle Trac...and Janie...help her not to be sad. Amen."

Trac's eyes felt moist as the sweet voice prayed with such innocence and belief. He wished he had the same ability.

Scurrying about as always, Trac watched his beloved middle sister, the sweetest-natured of the three and was glad she had married and stayed at the family ranch. Margaret had always been the beauty; high-minded, and well trained in the social graces, she had been willing to wait for a rich husband. Her husband had made a small fortune during the gold rush days and they had married and set off for Boston where he'd come from.

Margaret belonged in the East whereas Louisa, dark-haired and brown-eyed like their mother, belonged here on the ranch. She loved the mountains.

41

Molly had come along later in their folks' lives and was a half-half mix of strong-willed Margaret and soft-hearted Louisa. She was nearing fifteen, almost a woman herself. He and Louisa both knew that, after visiting Margaret, Molly would no doubt make up her mind whether she would be staying in the mountains of Montana or moving back to city life in Boston with her elder sister.

Chapter 10

A llowing a puff of air to swoosh from her lungs, Louisa seated herself and pulled a small piece of brown paper from a book she had just retrieved from the shelf. "Here is my list. I need a few supplies when you get into town. You'll have plenty of time since the stage is almost always late. And you should have room for your supplies and mine, if you stack everything just right. If you have a problem, just get what you can, starting at the top of the list, of course, and I'll be happy. But please," she looked into Trac's eyes pleadingly, "please pick out a bolt of calico print. Something in blue . . . anything but brown. The girls need dresses badly and I'll probably have lots of winter hours of sewing ahead of me." She looked away.

"I'll see to it." He laughed. His sister was nothing if not practical, then paused. "Emmett'll be back in the spring if he doesn't make it through the pass this winter, sis."

"I know." She whispered and rested her back against the chair.

Trac knew she wanted to say something else. "What is it?"

"Janie." She replied then sat silent.

"Louisa, I've never been good at reading or understanding emotions, mine or anyone else's." *And I have an especially hard time understanding the female emotions.* He raised his eyebrows and waited.

"You do just fine, Trac. With three sisters and two nieces you're surrounded with females." She smiled tenderly. "I was thinking...Janie might need supplies, too."

"Well, what do you want me to do about it?" Trac squirmed in his seat.

"Oh Trac. Surely you have talked to Janie since . . . since . . ."

"I haven't seen her, Louisa." He said pushing the chair back from the table, nearly toppling it in his haste. "And I don't intend to."

Louisa looked completely surprised.

"Look, Louisa, she hates me. Plain and simple. She blames me for Billy's death and she's right." He punched his Stetson his head and stomped out the door.

"My goodness." Was all that Louisa could think to say.

Once the girls were asleep for the night, Louisa took her shawl from the peg and made her way down to the bunkhouse. Coming through the back, she entered the kitchen.

"Wes, it smells so good in here. What'd you all have for supper?"

"Oh the usual. Beef, beans and cornbread – and baked apple pies." He winked. "Want a piece?"

"I'd love some of your pie. You make the best crust this side of the Mississippi River."

Wes pulled a whole pie out of the cupboard.

"Where's Trac?"

"He's in the office. He hasn't had his yet, so I'll get you both some."

"Good, then I can talk to him." Wes followed her with two of the best looking plates of pie Louisa had seen in a long while. No matter how good she made a supper, she still couldn't make crust as tender as Wes'.

"Yeah, come in." came the reply at her gentle knock.

Trac stood to his feet. "Anything wrong Louisa?"

"Oh no, you just forgot my list this afternoon." She handed it to him as she took a seat. Wes handed off their plates and shut the door on his way out.

"It's been so long since I've been down at the bunkhouse." She sighed.

"You've got your hands full up at the house." Trac reminded her and dug into his pie.

"It's good to come down, though. Brings back so many memories. Remember when we used to play in here while the hands were out on the range; jumping from bunk to bunk like wild boars?"

"And the time Margaret marched up to the house and told on us?" Trac smiled.

"We both got whoopings after pa found out we'd shot rocks through those two windows with the brand new sling he'd made you."

"I used to see that sling, hung high up on a nail in the barn. I think Pa put it there to remind me what I'd lost for disobeying." He laughed.

"Remember the chicken house? Seems like so long ago." Louisa gazed out the small window in Trac's office. "I'll never forget the switching we got for throwing perfectly good eggs at the barn. The awful stuff is still there. It never washed off."

"Yeah, you're the one who told. I was going to lie forever and you couldn't help but tell the truth." Trac smiled.

He looked at his sister, suddenly noticing that she was no longer the little girl he remembered, but a grown woman with two little girls of her own. And he, four years older, should be looking out for her, especially since that gold-chasing husband of hers was away. Trac's heart struck him.

Pushing the old ladder-back chair away from his father's desk, he propped his black booted feet on the table and finished off the pie. "Good pie."

"Wes is the best pie maker this side of the Mississippi." Louisa agreed.

"So you came down to bring the list?"

He let down his feet and walked to the small window, shoving his hands in his rear pockets as he stared out into the early evening. The gas lantern sat precariously on the corner of the desk. "What other reason did you come down, sis?"

She looked up and they shared a knowing smile. "You always know when I'm up to something."

"Not always."

"Today, when you said it was your fault Billy died. What did you mean?" she asked softly.

Trac thought for a few moments before answering. He was a man of few words, preferring to work hard rather than talk. "Just telling the truth."

"Truth? How did you come to that conclusion?"

"I killed Billy as if I'd taken a gun and shot him myself."

"Trac, you know that's not true."

Silence.

"Tell me what happened again, please."

He'd just as soon walk right out the door, but he owed his sister an explanation. They'd barely mentioned it since he'd brought Janie to her that night.

Trac told the story again, reminding her distinctly how he'd accepted the bet and even upped the ante to two nuggets, selling Billy's soul down the river.

"Nonsense," she puffed and stood to her feet. She was a full head shorter than he and once she landed her small fists at her hips he knew that was a sign that a full-fledged storm was coming. "You know yourself Billy would have ridden that stallion no matter what you said or did. He loved a challenge and he never turned one down no matter what the prize."

"I should have never offered the gold nugget, let alone raised it. I knew he'd try extra hard because he hated to lose and he wanted to surprise Janie for her birthday with plans for a new hacienda."

Louisa's hand flew to her mouth. "Oh dear, what is today? Janie's birthday is coming. Have we missed it, Trac?" his sister's face was almost comical.

She was completely horrified so Trac went around to his desk and pulled out an old calendar. He knew exactly what day she was referring to but did not want his sister to know.

"Janie's birthday is September 1ˢᵗ." Louisa said aloud. "Good thing you spoke of it, for I would have let it pass. We must do something special to let her know the world is still aright."

Louisa was up and pacing now.

"Bake her something. You're good at that." He offered.

"No, that's not the perfect gift."

Trac shrugged. *What was the perfect gift for a new widow?* He thought bitterly.

She tapped her finger at her chin. "I'll think of something. Yes, I have it." Louisa grabbed a pencil from the desktop and wrote furiously on her list and handed it back to him. "I've added one more thing to my list. Now don't you forget it." She placed her finger at her lips, deep in thought again.

He pocketed the list and went back to work while his sister paced, sat again and paced again, their former conversation apparently forgotten.

After a span of time, Trac had finally had enough. "Louisa, stop pacing."

"Oh dear, it's been too long, I have to get back to the house." He watched through the window to make sure she entered the house and then went back to work. *Sweet Louisa. Always thinking of someone else.*

After she was gone from the room, Trac picked up his Bible from the side table near his bed and opening the thin pages, read "If it be possible, as much as lieth in you, live peaceably with all men . . ." He went no further. Obviously God was talking to him about Janie. He slammed the Book shut and leaned his chair back on two legs and pondered how in the world he could do that.

The passage in Romans 12 shook him to the bone. Could anything be more clear? Running his hands through his thick, dark hair he stood, set his hat on his head, and went outdoors. It was late, too late to visit Janie; but somehow he had to try to talk to her and soon. Guilt was eating him up inside.

Standing outside in the cool evening air, he walked stretching his back, arms and legs, letting his mind work to convince himself of what he had to do. He couldn't avoid Janie forever

Chapter 11

Two days later, before dawn Trac grabbed some clean clothes and headed to the small creek that ran behind the bunkhouse. The water was cold as ice but he needed a good scrubbing. He undressed quickly and jumped in yelling out as soon as his body hit the water. He soaped up and rinsed off and stepped out, water sluicing down his shivering frame. Shaking profusely he dressed in dry clothes and combed his fingers through his long hair. He needed to get a trim and his beard was nearly a week old.

His hat was warm against his cold flesh. Briskly walking out to the barn he retrieved his mount and headed for Janie's. It was time he spoke with her.

He would be leaving in less than an hour to go the hundred miles to Helena to get supplies. Surely he could make decent conversation with her long enough to find out if she had need of anything.

The closer he came, the more his stomach knotted. Janie's hatred for him was so bitter he doubted he'd be able to get within a mile of her, just like that black stallion, but for his part he had to try.

Flipping the reins around a post he walked the few steps across the porch, his boots clicking loud in the early morning and knocked. He half expected Billy to come rushing out and clap him on the shoulders, and challenge him to a hunt in the woods. Swallowing hard, he realized anew how that would never happen again.

When she didn't answer, he knocked again and waited. No answer. The door wasn't latched. Suddenly alarm quickened his heart. Something was wrong. He knocked and yelled again, opening the door cautiously.

The fire was out and he heard a slight noise. Janie appeared in the bedroom doorway her clothes wrinkled and twisted, her long hair disheveled. She rubbed her eyes against the sunlight that was streaming in the door behind him. Quickly he closed the door and her eyes focused.

"What are *you* doing here?" Her voice was hoarse, bitter.

Her hard look told him in an instant that he was not going to get anywhere with her, so he took the offensive.

"Why is your door unlatched?"

Stiff arms criss-crossed over her chest.

"Well, latch it when you sleep. I'm going to Helena. You need anything?"

She stared angrily then said, "Why, you feeling guilty?"

Seeing he was going to get nowhere he turned on his heel and quit the cabin. *You can just stay here for all I care.* The thought crashed through his mind. Janie had always kept herself beautiful and her home neat. The cabin was a mess and so was she. *Because Billy's not here.* Intense guilt snagged his conscience.

"Latch the door, Janie. Anyone could just walk in." He called out loudly over his shoulder and turned Job toward home.

Janie picked up the closest object, which happened to be the matchbox and hurled it at the door before she fell into a heap sobbing, "I hate you, Trac Cordera. I hate you."

Back at his barn Trac hitched up the horses to the wagon and started down the trail alone with plenty of time to think. It would take him several days to get to Helena, without trouble. A secret compartment underneath the wagon bed hid his paper money and a nugget of gold.

The day passed and glad to be alone, he stopped to make a small fire and eat. Pulling his slicker over his shoulders, for lightning was already showing in the south, he dug a ditch on either side to catch the rain and slept under the wagon. Rain pelted the wagon bed for an hour or so, but the ground remained dry.

* * *

After the girls had gone to bed, Louisa sat down by lamplight to write Emmett:

Molly's not coming home until spring and so we were hoping that we might see you before the snow closes the pass this winter, my dear Emmett. All your girls miss you. Janie is still inconsolable. It's been a grievous time for us all. I wish you were here.

Trac went for supplies today. I am anxious to hear word from Margaret, too, as I'm certain she and Molly are having good times together back east.Virginia is growing so much and is helpful with little Grace, who is also getting chubby and is so loving like her sister. I've sent a curl from Grace's hair Have you found your gold yet? We await your return anxiously.

Your loving wife, Louisa

Louisa was displeased with herself for not penning the letter sooner, so Trac could have carried it to Helena with him, but truth to tell, she'd barely had a free moment to herself these past weeks. The chores had to be done and Trac was busy with Janie's place. And there were the visits to Janie every few days. Louisa found her to be in the same condition time after time. She was barely eating and the cabin was in shambles but Janie got angry each time she tried to pick up or fix her something to eat. Louisa feared Janie would go to her own grave if she didn't come out of her grief soon.

Trac had left earlier that morning, long before her and the girls had risen. Now her letter was done. She could send one of the ranch hands into Stonewall where it would be picked up within the week. Satisfied she hustled the girls around, promising Virginia a visit to Janie's house.

Already Louisa was dreading her decision. Although she remained bright and happy for her children's sake she wondered at the sensibilities of letting her eldest witness the wretched affair. But unable to do anything about it, the obligation to care for Janie in Billy's absence foremost, she drove herself over in the wagon and knocked at the door.

The latch was not in place so she called and entered. Janie was still abed. At least she had on night clothes, which Louisa noted were twisted and wrinkled.

"Janie." She called quietly from the doorway. "Me and the girls are here to see you."

No answer. After a few minutes Grace fussed to nurse so she sat in the rocker and quieted the baby while surveying the work she would do once she was finished feeding her daughter.

"Virginia dear, won't you gather up the stockings and things and pile them near the front door. Away from the fire. There's a good girl."

Grace safely asleep on her pallet, Louisa set the house to rights again and put on a pot to make tea.

"Who's there?"

"It's me and the girls, Janie. I've made tea and lunch is ready. Come eat with us." Louisa called gaily.

"I'm not hungry."

Virginia stood in the doorway looking at Janie. "Please come out and eat with us. Mama made something good. She even brought berry jam." The child smiled shyly. "For your birthday."

Janie looked up and seeing the child's pleading face, burst into tears.

"Whatever is wrong?" Louisa came running.

"Nothing. Nothing. Just leave me alone, please. I don't want to see anyone just now." Janie cried out and threw herself back upon the disheveled bed.

Louisa's hands went to her hips. "Now Janie, I've had myself a bellyful of your sassiness. Get yourself out of that bed and put on a dress. You are going to eat. This is your birthday." She turned on her heel and Virginia followed her mother meekly.

Janie dragged herself out of the bed and threw her gown up and over her head. She nearly gagged at the smell of the food. It had been so long since she'd eaten more than a biscuit here and there, the smells made her stomach lurch. She threw on a pair of underthings, her chemise, and the oldest dress she could lay her hands on. It was faded and worn, just like she felt.

When she appeared in the doorway, Louisa held back the look of surprise on her face. "Sit here, I'll get you some tea. You have no more sugar in the house so we'll have to drink it plain, I'm afraid." She spoke nonchalantly as she set a cup at her place.

Janie plopped heavily onto a chair and picked up the teacup. Louisa noted her shaking hands as she did so, but thinking better than to mention it, prepared a biscuit and a bit of her own churned butter and set in on the table in front of her. As soon as she did Janie jumped up and wretched outside the back door. Her stomach must have been empty because all Louisa heard was the dry heaves.

"Come inside, dear. A cup of tea with no sugar will set your stomach right again. Here sip, but don't gulp." She said tenderly.

Janie's face was red and blotchy. She picked up the cup and sipped. Before long she could sit no longer and went back to her bed. Virginia began to weep.

"Darling, whatever is the matter?"

"Aunt Janie is so sick, Mama, she can't even drink her tea."

"Yes, dear, but she will get well. You and I will help her, won't we?"

"Yes, Mama."

Janie heard the exchange and felt a stab of guilt. She was behaving so badly even Virginia was crying. Too tired and too sick to think about it, she chose to turn over and sleep.

Louisa finished cleaning up, and left a small plate of beans and bread in the warming oven, and headed home. "We'll wash these clothes and bring 'em back another day." She spoke to Virginia, hoping to set the child's heart right again.

While Virginia's head bounced against her side, and Grace slept in a box right behind the seat, she prayed, *Lord I don't know what to do. Please help Janie and help me be a good friend to her. I don't know what my heart would do if we lost her, too.*

"Mama, is it okay to ask the Lord to *make* Janie all right even if she doesn't want to?" Virginia's question astounded her, for indeed she had no answer and said so.

A moment later, hearing nothing from her eldest, she glanced over and found her daughter's dark head bent over, her tiny lips moving. Louisa's heart melted. She hoped always that her children would turn to the Lord in time of need.

Lord, please bless Virginia's prayer.

Chapter 12

The days flew by and soon Louisa heard the sound of Trac's wagon as it pulled up in front of the ranch. She threw open the door and called over her shoulder, "Virginia, come, Uncle Trac's home!"

Before the wagon had come to a stop Louisa was at Trac's side. "Did the trip go well?"

"Fine." Trac jumped off the seat and groaned as he muscled a large wooden box toward the back of the wagon. "I've got letters from Emmet." He pulled the crumpled treasures from his pocket and handed them to her.

"Two of them. Oh my." Louisa grabbed them and went into the house and then to her bedroom, shutting the door.

"C'mon Virginia, I've got something for you." He swept his niece up into his arms.

"Just like Daddy." She giggled as he dropped her onto the wagon bed and pointed to a package. "Over there in the corner. The one with the yellow ribbon tied around it."

"This one, Uncle Trac?" she said and lifted the brown paper package.

"That's the one. It's yours." He smiled as her bright eyes sought his permission to open. "Open it." he laughed as he carried in boxes of supplies and dropped them on Louisa's table.

"Uncle Trac it's for a new dress . . . for mama?"

"Nope, that one's for you! Time you learned to sew as good as your ma." He watched as she held up the small piece of fabric he'd chosen just for her. "The other length is for Grace a dress just like her big sister's."

Virginia smiled and he was satisfied.

When he was finished and still hadn't seen Louisa, he crouched down to catch Virginia's eyes, "Watch out for Grace. I'll be down at the bunkhouse."

By the time he and Wes had finished unloading the rest of the supplies, he saw Louisa coming down the hill. She was crying.

"Come on, we'll talk in my office." He led her there and sat down on the edge of the desk, preparing himself for more bad news. "What's wrong?" he leaned forward, elbows on his knees.

"It's Emmett." Trac waited for her to get her bearings.

"He's not coming home." She cried softly. "First Molly and now Emmett."

"Then he's not dead?" Trac let out a breath.

"Dead? No, but he's not coming home." She made a pass at the tears with the back of her hand.

"Louisa, I'm sorry. What is the reason?" he asked more kindly.

"He's found a new vein of gold and he can't leave the dig for fear that someone might take it over whilst he's gone."

"Oh, then that's good news, right?" he encouraged.

"Yes, I suppose." She agreed, but Trac knew she did so reluctantly.

"Your husband is safe and he's found a vein. Perhaps he'll be rich someday."

Louisa smiled through her tears. "Trac you always help me look on the good side. I only wish you'd do it for yourself."

Her words hit him hard. She was right. He was full of good words and encouragement for everyone else, yet had not given his guilt to the only One who knew what to do with it. The only way he could assuage his conscience would be to shut his feelings for Janie out of his heart and go on as though she were his sister, not the woman he had always secretly loved. No one had ever known and no one ever would.

Seeing his sister suffer over Emmett . . . and how Janie was suffering over losing Billy . . . he knew he did not want a woman crying over him some day and thought it best never to take a wife.

Perhaps then he could get on with his life and Janie hers. Somehow he would need to deal with the situation. It wasn't going to go away. Janie had hardened her heart and he could do it too and do it well.

Louisa saw the severe determination on his tanned face as he wrestled with what she knew he would never get over. She dearly loved that face. Dark eyes, so black they would frighten you if you did not know his kindheartedness. Dark, almost black hair, like their father's and strong muscles. He was a handsome man, but most of all he was a good-hearted man.

Trac meant the world to her, especially now with her husband gone. Sadness left her feeling bereft since she so longed to see Emmett and had hoped he would be home any day. How long the winter would be without him and Molly.

"Have you seen Janie?" Trac asked.

"Yes, but she's no better, Trac. She lives in her bed and the house is always a mess. I washed her and Billy's clothes, but it's near useless since she hardly bothers changing. And I've got Billy's things. I was wondering what to do with them." She sighed, still melancholy.

Trac surprised himself by saying, "I'll take them to her."

"Oh Trac do you think it wise? I had thought to keep them in my trunks so the…memories…you know."

"Memories are what's important, Louisa. She needs those memories if she's going to get better. I'll pick up Billy's things and make a trip over there. I have a few supplies for her and that would be a good reason to visit."

"I'll go up and get them, check on the girls. But I warn you, Trac, she's no different."

"I'll handle her." Today he would begin his new approach. In his mind Janie no longer held his heart.

Louisa looked into her brother's eyes. She stood on tiptoe and kissed his dark whiskered cheek. "Thank you, Trac. I'm so glad you're here for me and the girls."

Trac smiled that crooked smile and Louisa giggled. "You are just like a little boy yourself." She teased.

"The more mothering I get." He winked. "Left something up at the house for you."

With that Louisa hurried out of the bunkhouse. He heard the door slam. *Women love gifts.*

Trac finished working the account books, checked Janie's supplies, then headed up to the house.

"Tracson Gage Cordera – why didn't you tell me you were buying this?" she pointed to the Singer sewing machine, the wooden box it arrived in, open and in shreds.

"Thought you might like to sew something for the girls this winter." He shrugged, the hint of a smile on his weathered face.

"I've already got lots of ideas. Why I can make the girls' dresses for the church Christmas recital and sew for Janie and Mrs. Preston needs new curtains for her kitchen, not to mention —"

"Whoa, Nellie," he held up his hands. "It's getting near dark and I need to get these supplies over to Janie's. Got Billy's things you want me to drop off?"

"Yes, but first..." she reached up and kissed her brother's cheek again. "I'll bake you two pies next week, as soon as I can get some time."

"Thanks. Nothing I'd like better." He took the clothes Louisa had sitting in a neat pile.

"Everything's mended." She fingered Billy's denim vest. "It was his favorite." She said softly. "I really miss him, too, Trac." Tears popped into her eyes and she turned to busy herself, then turned back after she'd collected her emotions. "Billy was family, Trac, but more than that I know he was your best friend."

Trac pulled on his hat and cleared his throat.

They shared a look and Louisa heard Grace whimpering. "I have to go." She whispered. "I'll pray for your visit to Janie's" and hurried to feed her child.

Chapter 13

Trac drove the wagon slowly through the pasture path, preferring to stay off the main road, which was dusty. As he approached her house he saw Janie standing by the line of cottonwood trees. She didn't run as he drove up and didn't turn toward him either. *The wind must be in her ears.* She had on a dress and her hair was swept up, not running wild and loose like it had been. He hardened his heart.

"I've brought your supplies." His voice was gruff.

"I didn't ask for supplies." She stated smugly, never bothering to turn.

"Louisa did." He returned and jumped down. "Where do you want them?"

"I don't care."

Without another word Trac unloaded the few supplies, dumped them on her trestle table near the hearth. He gathered up hers and Billy's clothes and lay them in her rocker then quit the cabin. As the wagon rumbled away he felt childish, but there was nothing to say to someone who hated you so bitterly. Nothing at all.

For a week Trac pressed himself into whatever task he could find to do. He assisted two females in calving their yearlings and wrestled with a new barn door by himself since the men were out gathering strays again where a section of rotted fence posts were run down by a small stampede.

"Wes," he called out. "Mind helping me with something down at the barn?" he growled one afternoon. Wes came out, wiping his hands on the oversized white apron covering his overalls. "Yeah, boss, what is it?"

"Got this table I been working on and darn thing's so heavy, I can't get it on the wagon bed."

"C'mon boss, I got supper to make and you know the guys don't take too kindly to waitin' on supper."

Trac laughed and agreed.

Wes grabbed his hat and snapped it on his head, smiling. "By golly, now ye're sounding like yer own self agin'." He walked a little faster.

Trac led the way and before they got to the barn, heard a wail. "One o'them is calving."

Trac and Wes hurried inside. "Didn't know we were expecting any more," Trac said and walked toward the sound. "Sure enough. It's Old Sally."

"Well, ain't that somthin', her as old as she is an all."

Trac knelt on one knee and saw immediately Old Sally was in trouble. "Coming out backwards." He said over his shoulder. "It's going to be a long, hard delivery. I'll stay here, you go on back to the bunkhouse, get the guys supper. We'll load the table another day."

"Right, boss."

"Thanks, Wes." Another moan from the stall brought Trac's attention back to the job at hand. "Old Sally, it's just you and me." He patted the animal's side and big brown eyes rolled back to see who was attending her.

Hours passed and Old Sally got worse. Twice Louisa had come down to the barn to check on him and Old Sally, but nothing was going on except he could see the animal was going to wear out before she could get her calf birthed.

"Time to get tough, old girl. Sorry. Can't afford to lose both of you."

Trac rolled up the sleeves of his shirt and sat down, then placed both booted feet on Old Sally's behind and took hold of the only hoof he could grab onto and pulled and pulled until the calf came sliding out on the hay. "Whoa, we got her Old Sal. You did it."

Old Sally lifted her head and moaned then laid it back down.

"You worked for this one. Now don't go getting yourself in trouble again, you hear?" he patted the animal's side and watched as nature took her course, mother and daughter bonding. Within the hour the calf was trying to get up and walk. Old Sally just lay there.

Finished, Trac washed up and rolled down his sleeves, grabbed the old lantern and headed down to the bunkhouse. It was already dark.

"Well, how'd it go? Old Sal make it?" Wes wanted to know.

"She sure did. Got herself a daughter...and at her age, too." Trac smiled. "Supper still waiting?" He removed his shirt, tossed it on a nail, scrubbed up to his elbows and put on a fresh shirt.

"Yep, right here in the warming oven. Big beefsteak and potatoes with lots of butter and milk mashed in."

"Great. I'm starved. Everyone in for the night?"

"Yep. Oh yeah, almost forgot, some new guy came sashayin' in here wantin' work. Some youngun, thinking he was a man." Wes snubbed his nose. "At least that was my opinion."

"What was his name?"

"Kid by the name o' Matthew O'Hearn."

"O'Hearn. Isn't that the big O'H Ranch other side of Helena?"

"Ya got me. Acts like he thinks he's somebody." Wes shrugged. "Says he'll be back tomorra."

"Pretty late in the season to be looking for work." He wondered. "I'll see him when he comes. We need an outrider, Pistol's heading home. His wife is having their sixth and he wants to be there for this one." Trac smiled. "Since he missed all the others."

"Pistol oughta go on home. He ain't been there for nine months!"

Trac and Wes shared a smile. Pistol could be gone home for one month and his wife would be in the family way again.

"Bout time he went back and helped her raise all them young'uns, you ask me." Wes tossed his comments over his shoulder.

Trac smiled and ate.

"Good victuals, Wes. Man that was good." Trac patted his flat stomach and stood, stretching. "You going to Sunday church tomorrow?"

"Yeah." Wes gave him a look.

"Just askin'." Trac winked at his cook. He was sweet on Mrs. Preston and everybody knew it.

"I'm turning in.

Next morning came and Trac was bathed and ready to go. "C'mon Wes you look spiffy enough. Girls are waitin' up at the ranch."

"Now you watch your tongue. I'm your elder." He warned, twisting his long white mustache. "'Sides, you're looking pretty good yourself, for a young whippersnapper."

"Cow hand." Trac pulled on his best black vest over a clean white shirt and knotted a black string tie at his neck, then loosened it.

"Janie comin'?" Wes asked.

Trac looked him in the eye trying to read his true question. "What do you think?"

Wes shrugged. "Just wonderin's all."

Trac realized he was probably asking because he was sweet on Janie's mother.

Ten minutes later Trac was waiting out front for Louisa and the girls to come out. Wes had already hopped down from the wagon to knock on the door.

"Looks like we might have a nice day." Wes squinted up at the sky

A long, low whistle rang out in the early morning as Louisa and the girls came out in their new dresses, all three. "Whoa, what have we here?" Wes winked and whistled louder than Trac.

"Oh, now, no funny stuff, boys. Virginia and I worked hard to get these dresses done for Sunday church. But that Singer sewing machine sure helped us along. Why I had no trouble at all." She smiled at Trac and patted his arm as she settled next to her brother. Wes handed Grace up.

"I'll ride back here with the young'un." Wes jumped up in the back after spreading a blanket over the straw. "We'll mind the tail."

Virginia giggled as she settled herself next to Wes and Trac clicked his tongue. The wagon jerked forward.

"Next year, Lord willing, I hope we have church closer. Reverend Dunham says we'll be needing something this side of the pass before long, since the church has barely got room for all the folks now."

"That'll sure be nice." Wes agreed.

"Way it is now, when winter comes, we'll miss church for months." Louisa sighed. "All the more reason to get a new church, this side of the pass."

Trac was lost in thought, wondering if Janie would be all right at her cabin. Most of the men were in town for the weekend and that meant she was pretty much on her own. Settling his Stetson lower against the rising sun, he mentally figured how many cattle they'd bring back in the spring.

The wagon moved slowly over the rain-washed dirt. "Nice day." Louisa smiled. "At least the dust is not getting in the girls' eyes. Trees are already starting to turn. I hardly noticed." She gazed out over the land.

"You heard any more from Emmett?" Trac asked.

"No, but my heart tells me we'll hear this week." Louisa's tentative smile warned Trac that he was on delicate territory, so he turned his attentions to driving.

They rode in silence, Trac thinking about the legacy the Cordera brothers had left him and Billy. As young and crazy cousins they'd talked and planned on marrying and having a whole passel of kids to help work the side-by-side ranches. Billy was usually the first to live out his dreams. For that, Trac was grateful. At least Billy had loved and been loved.

Now Trac's 160 acres and Billy's 200 was more than he could handle. The cattle business had been lucrative for their fathers and had left the boys well enough off, but there was so much work to be done, Trac knew he'd have to oversee Janie's ranch, Mrs. Preston's and his own. Billy had taken care of Mrs. Preston's place. It was only 10 acres, but still needed much in the way of repair. He'd have to hire more men, even if there wasn't going to be much more income coming in, especially at Billy's place. Perhaps he'd best talk to Janie about selling off some of the acres, keeping only a few for herself.

If he bought her herd, it'd bring in enough cash to last her a lifetime, and Trac wouldn't have to hire riders, buy feed, keep the fences and barns in shape. He could pay her rent to use her existing pastures. She wouldn't have to lift a finger.

* * *

Louisa thought about Emmett, wishing he saw cattle farming as a good way of life like her brother. Emmett hated cattle ranching and wished for a fancy house sitting high on a hill with lights burning in all the windows. And to be mayor of Stonewall.

"Wish Emmett were here with us today." She voiced her thoughts. "'Course he'd be thinking about building a fancy house high on a hill, wantin' to run for mayor."

She laughed, but Trac knew not in joy.

"You know Emmett, Lou. He's gotta have the best, be the best, nothing wrong with that."

"I know. He's so handsome and friendly with everyone he meets he'll have no trouble becoming the town politician."

"Yep, that's the way he is."

Louisa said nothing, remembering how she'd lost her heart to Emmett the moment she laid eyes on him. She missed him sorely. Grace possessed the image of her father's dark red hair and that only made her more lonely for her husband.

"Still thinking of Emmett?" Trac's gaze slid sideways.

"Yes, how did you know?"

"You have a certain look on your face, sis."

"You know me too well, brother." She patted his arm and changed Grace's position.

Church services ended too soon for Louisa and not soon enough for Trac. He checked his timepiece. Just enough time before dark set in to get chores done. Mrs. Preston had informed him at church that her foreman was called away home. Something about a sick child. He'd need extra hands today.

"Wait Trac, I must speak to Mrs. Bern." His sister hurried away, promising to return quickly.

Trac waited by the wagon. Wes and Mrs. Preston talked quietly under a huge Oak while Virginia ran with several other little girls. About the time he'd run out of patience, he heard the rustle of skirts and turned.

"Miss Denton."

"Delaney, remember Trac?" The blond-haired woman smiled from beneath her blue bonnet.

"Ma'am." He said quietly and removed his hat, smoothing his dark hair back, ignoring her request. He'd mistakenly addressed her by her Christian name once.

"Haven't seen you about for quite some time." She spoke with a very proper eastern accent.

"Got a ranch to run." He looked out over the land, gazing back once or twice.

"I'm very sorry about Billy." She said quietly.

"Thanks." He mumbled not taking his eyes off the horizon. "Been taking care of Billy's place."

"Yes, I know." She paused. "Seems I remember a certain promise you made me sometime ago."

Trac turned remembering instantly. "Sorry, Miss Denton, I had forgotten."

"Delaney." She reminded him again. "Perhaps we can remedy that. The church is having a supper on the grounds Sunday next. Perhaps you'd be my escort?"

Trac put his hat on, looked down at the pretty blue-eyed woman standing in front of him and knew he couldn't refuse. He'd forgotten he'd promised to take her to the barn dance more than a month ago.

He also knew the talk of the town, after he'd taken Miss Delaney Denton, out riding again, it would be understood, Trac was courting her.

She was the banker's daughter. What was he supposed to do? Ignore her? He'd taken her riding at her father's suggestion.

Twice. That was months ago, but he knew the ladies in the territory. They'd consider it a near betrothal if he didn't watch it.

"I'd be honored, Miss Denton." He refused to call a lady by her Christian name, especially at church where folks might overhear and assume more than he intended.

"Why thank you. I knew you would honor your promise. I look forward to next week, then." She smiled coyly and then she was off, a puff of lilac fragrance left in her wake.

Trac pulled his hat on and wished he'd stayed at the ranch. He hadn't been to church much in the last several months, summer was too busy and then when Billy died he hadn't wanted to sit under the minister's preaching compounding the blasted conviction he carried. He knew he should talk to God, but all he could think to say was *why*, just like Janie had shouted at him that day, fists flailing. For a moment he understood Janie's bitterness.

Chapter 14

"Come Virginia, Uncle Trac is ready to go." Louisa rounded up her child and with Grace on her hip, was trying to muscle a large package. Trac reached for it.

"No, here take Grace." She said and angled her hip. I'll get the package."

Trac saw his sister's face turn red and couldn't help but wonder what had ruffled her feathers.

"Thanks," she murmured and hurried to place the parcel beneath a blanket. Trac shrugged and chucked Grace under her chin and she buried her face in his shoulder shyly.

"She's getting big." Trac smiled down at the chubby face, the blue eyes like her father's. Emmett's missing a whole lot back home." Then was instantly sorry for saying anything, for Louisa's countenance fell. "Sorry, sis."

"It's okay, Trac. I'll make it. Next week we've got supper on the grounds, if the weather holds." She said quietly. "And I'll have plenty of work to do before that."

"Good." With one hand Trac helped Virginia get into the back of the wagon. "Here, hold your sister til your Ma gets up." Trac helped his sister up to the seat next to him and reached for Grace.

She howled and he handed her to her mother. "Hungry again?" he said.

"Always." Louisa prepared herself to feed her child.

His gaze circled the horizon. "I'll get Wes."

Before long the group was headed toward home. "Mrs. Preston come by herself?" Trac asked.

"What's it to you?" Wes' angry reply surprised him.

"Just wondered, if we ought to wait around and take the trail back together." Trac said easily, wondering what was in the air.

"Aw, go on...she rode with that old Mr. Tomkins. Feeble old..."

"Watch your language." Louisa warned quietly.

"Better than riding all this way alone." Trac smiled gazing over the countryside.

They rode in silence for sometime, before Louisa spoke.

"You thinking about asking Mrs. Preston to the church supper next week, Wes?"

Wes took his time in answering, Trac noted.

"Thinkin' on it."

"Well, I think you'd better do more'n think about it. I heard the ladies talking today. Old Mr. Tomkins is thinking on asking Mrs. Preston for her hand."

"What?" Wes shouted. "Why that old geezer, he ain't good enough ta . . . ta plant her corn, let alone marry up with a fine woman like her." His eyes fluttered downward to Virginia's brown-eyed gaze and said no more.

"Want me to sew you a new shirt for next week, Wes?" Louisa changed the topic.

"Think you'd have time?"

"I'll make time." She threw back over her shoulder. "But just for you."

After awhile Wes spoke quietly, "You think it might help?"

"I sure do. You've been wearing that same shirt to church ever since I can remember." Louisa never looked back, but knew Wes was looking down at that old shirt.

"You could be right at that..."

"I have some material left over from sewing Emmett's shirts. Fine material. And now that I have my sewing machine, I can whip off one in no time."

"I thank ya." Wes returned, just minutes before he was asleep and snoring, Virginia asleep under his arm.

"You coming next week, Trac?" Louisa talked quietly, the sun high.

"Yeah."

"You don't sound very happy about it. You need some time away. I know you're trying to take care of Janie's ranch and Mrs. Preston's place, Trac and sure as I'm sitting here you're gonna collapse, especially with so many of the men heading home for winter.

"It's got to be done, Louisa. That's all there is to it."

"Do you have to be the one to do it, Trac?"

The question burned a hole in his conscience.

"Janie can hire a foreman. He can stay down at the bunkhouse with your men and run her place, pure and simple. He could help at Mrs. Preston's too, earn his wage."

Trac didn't answer. He knew what she said was true. Besides, he'd already appointed a foreman, but the man drank too much. He didn't want him hanging around Janie's place, her there alone. Men would be wanting a pretty thing like her with a big ranch as part of the bundle.

"I'm telling you Trac, you have a life of your own to live."

Trac wanted to shout at her, *I don't want one. Billy can't have one. I don't want one.* He kept his peace choosing to gaze out over the land, rather than face Louisa.

"Why don't you at least talk to Janie."

"She doesn't have anything to say to me, Louisa. You know that."

"Well, you two have to talk sometime." She shot back.

Trac knew that if his sister were standing, she'd have her hands on her hips.

"A hundred years from now is soon enough for me." He slapped the reins.

"God will work everything out, Trac. But you have to trust Him."

Louisa, so like their mother.

* * *

The week passed all too soon and it was Saturday night and raining. Trac was having a bath in his office.

"Think we'll make it tomorra?" Wes poured another kettle of boiling water into the cool bath.

"Ouch. Watch it will ya?" Trac shouted.

"Sorry, boss, just thinkin'."

"Why don't you just go on over and ask Mrs. Preston to ride in with you and Louisa tomorrow." Trac muttered, the skin on his forearm burning. "And watch where you pour that hot water next time."

"You 'spose that old geezer's already done the askin'?"

"Only one way to find out. Go on. Git." Trac waved him off. "Give me some peace will ya?"

Wes set the empty kettle on the stove and snatched it up again before the bottom could burn, then dropped it to the floor, the handle burning his hand. It clattered like a church bell echoing over the hillside.

"Guess I'd better go on over." He muttered. "You think Louisa's got that shirt done?"

"Well, I'll be darned if I'd know about it if she did." Trac looked at his cook.

"Right."

Trac heard the door slam.

"Women." He growled and ducked his shampooed head under water. He had his own problems without worrying about Wes' too. Miss Delaney Denton awaited his arrival tomorrow morning before church and he wasn't the least excited. *Maybe it'll rain all night. Hard.*

But morning brought bright sunshine and a brisk wind.

"Wes you remember you're supposed to haul Louisa and the girls to church."

"Yeah, I know it."

"You sound pretty happy this morning. Louisa get your shirt done?"

"She shore did. Lookee here." Wes came to his office door.

Trac was truly shocked. "Where'd all your hair go? You look like a brand new calf right out of its mother."

"Aw, don't be given me trouble. 'Sides ain't no business o'yours. Just 'cause you're my boss, don't mean . . ."

Trac couldn't help but smile. "You're right about that." Trac waited a decent amount of time and asked, "So who did the honors?"

A long pause followed and Trac heard the banging of pots in the kitchen.

"Miz. Preston." Came the reply minutes later.

Trac had a tough time not bursting out in a guffaw. Instead he allowed himself a chuckle under his breath, then realized it was the first time he'd had any inclination to laugh since Billy died.

"I heered that." Came from the kitchen.

Trac could not speak, if he did he would lose what control he did have. Wes, courting a woman. He'd known Wes since he was knee high to him and he'd never married, never been with a woman, far as he knew.

"But for the grace of God go I." He muttered and lifted himself from his chair, checked his nicked chin in the mirror, smoothed his hair one last time. *Next time you make a promise, you'd best think twice.* "See you after church, Wes, you drive the girls careful, now."

"You just see to yourself, cowboy." Wes shouted back.

Trac tucked his new white shirt into the best pair of brown pants he owned, added his cowhide vest, then went to the barn for the fancy carriage, changed his mind and chose the small wagon. *Can't make it look like I'm a serious caller.* Then he felt guilty.

Miss Denton was a good-looking woman and her father was the town banker. He could ill afford to make Mr. Denton his enemy, but didn't exactly feel like a gentleman, either, courting Miss Denton when he didn't have the slightest intention of seeing her again.

Chapter 15

The wagon rattled over the ruts. Glad to be alone, Trac meandered, shot a rattler that had the horses nearly out of control, and arrived in town sooner than he wished. He pulled the small wagon up to the Denton home and tied the horse to the hitching post. In moments he'd walked through the short white picket fence and was banging the knocker shaped like a horseshoe against the heavy door.

"Mr. Cordera. Please come in."

"Mrs. Denton, Trac removed his hat and nodded.

"Delaney is upstairs, finishing her dress. She'll be right down. Have a seat in the parlor. I'll get Mr. Denton." She walked him to the small room and disappeared. He sat on the largest chair, avoiding the settee for two.

"Why Tracson Cordera, haven't talked to you in quite some time. Sure was hard hearing about Billy." He shook his head. "And so young, with a wife, too."

Trac nodded.

"How're things going at the ranch?" This from Mr. Denton.

Trac stood and held his hat in front of him. "Good." He answered quietly.

"Sit, son. I hear you've come for my daughter."

"Yes sir." Trac sat down again.

The older man, tossed the tails on his coat and seated himself on the settee. "Mrs. Denton and I will be attending the church supper today. It's a mighty nice day after all." He said quietly.

"Yes sir." Miss Denton appeared in the doorway and Trac stood.

"Mr. Cordera." She dipped her head slightly and waited.

"Ready, then?" he offered his elbow.

"Father, tell mother I'm off. Oh I almost forgot..." she ran to another room and came back with a box. "My special pie. Blackberry."

"Sounds good." Trac smiled. "Shall we?" he accepted the package and offered his other arm.

Her father, standing now, winked and Trac could hear the older man's booted feet cross the room behind them. "We'll see you there." Mr. Denton waved and was gone.

Trac opened the door and stepped aside. "Miss Denton." He offered and let her pass, put his hat on and helped her up into the wagon "I'll put the pie in back for safekeeping."

"Your carriage is broken?" she asked sweetly, gathering her skirts.

"No." he answered truthfully and let the matter alone.

"I see." She said and cleared her throat.

Trac flicked the horses and they jolted forward. Miss Denton grabbed for her hat before the wind and the jerk of the horses could relieve her of it.

"Sorry, they're a little spooked. Met up with a rattler on the way." He said by way of explanation.

She looked sideways at him and frowned. "I hate snakes."

"You and me both, Miss Denton."

"Must you continue to call me Miss Denton?" she asked.

Trac didn't know what to say at first. "My sister would feel she had to teach me my manners all over again if she heard me call you by your Christian name."

"Well, it's not that we haven't been out together before." She suggested sweetly and gave him her best smile.

Exactly what I was afraid of. How long will it be before everybody's talking after today?

"Look, Miss Denton, I will be busy, real busy these next few months, maybe even years. I've got two ranches to run. I think it might be best if..."

"What, if I found someone else to bother?" she looked slighted.

"That's not what I was going to say." He stated firmly.

"Well then?"

"I . . . like I said, I'll be busy. Too busy to court a woman the proper way." He said quietly.

"Which is to say, you do not wish to see me again?"

"You are a beautiful woman. And you deserve the right to know the truth." Trac was surprised at his own words.

"And you are a good man, Tracson Cordera. I had hoped . . ." she stopped, blushing at her own words.

He glanced sideways and saw that she was looking away from him and he could see she was having difficulty with her emotions. He had hurt her.

"I am truly sorry, if I offended you, Miss Denton." He was careful to be kind, for above all things he hated to see a woman cry.

She nodded slightly, but kept her face averted. The day had started badly. When long moments passed without words, Trac finally declared. "Shall we be friends, then."

"As you wish." Her words were quiet.

Dreading the rest of the day, he snapped the reins wishing to end the day as soon as possible.

Miss Denton grabbed the sideboards and held on.

When they began to get closer, she sat up straighter. Wagons were coming from all directions and already the noise of the crowd could be heard echoing through the valley. "Well if that don't beat all." Trac smiled. "Look at Wes driving Mrs. Preston."

Delaney Denton smiled and Trac thought again how beautiful she was. And kind. She had already forgotten. He watched as she lifted her hand and waved as several couples passed in their wagons.

"Look, Louisa and the girls are in back." She said.

Trac waved. "Louisa brought her lemon cake." Louisa was right. It was time to go easy, enjoy the day. He set one booted foot up against the front board and slowed the horses.

"Over there are the tables. Perhaps you could stop and let me drop off my pie."

He pulled the wagon in line and watched each man get down and set baskets of food on the table and continue on. He did the same.

"Would you like to wait here while I park the wagon?" he offered.

"Yes, thank you."

Trac noted the lightness of her weight as he lifted her down.

She smiled as he jumped back on the seat and pulled away. Near a stand of trees he parked the wagon and curried the horses. "Whoa... girl." He whispered. He brought the basket of oats from the wagon, fed them and walked to the grounds.

"Mr. Cordera. How nice to see you again. We haven't seen much of you lately." Mrs. Bern said kindly. Trac could see she wanted to say more. "We miss Billy, too. And Janie."

Trac's eyes shuttered the grief he felt burning in his own heart and realized it was small compared to the pain he felt in his conscience. "Thank you Mrs. Bern. We all miss Billy, most of all Janie."

"Yes, dear. But time will heal the heart. It won't forget, but it will heal."

Trac knew she spoke out of experience. Mrs. Bern had already buried two husbands in this wild Montana Territory.

"Yes ma'am."

"If God didn't know what He was doing, we'd all be in a peck a'trouble." She smiled. "C'mon now let's find Miss Denton. She sure is a pretty one." Mrs. Bern took hold of Trac's arm and led the way.

"Miss Denton, I've found him for you." She winked and left the two alone.

"Thank you Mrs. Bern." Delaney's too-quiet response had Trac looking into her face.

"Hungry?" he asked and took her arm. "Let's find Lolly Mae Winger's chicken." He smiled.

After they had both eaten they found Mr. and Mrs. Denton. They were walking together until one of the bank's employee's, Ellis Bernard, came up and started talking to Mr. Denton. The two men had moved away to talk quietly and Trac saw Mrs. Denton standing alone.

"Would you like to ask your mother to join us under a tree?" Trac asked quietly.

"Of course." She whispered, walking ahead. "Mother, would you like to join us. Trac has a quilt."

"Actually, I'll have to see if Louisa brought an extra one...I didn't think..." He invited the ladies to wait for him and went off to look for his sister.

"Uncle Trac" Virginia called and ran to him. He ducked just quick enough to catch her as she barreled into him. "Whoa...take it easy, little sister."

"I was just running to get my stick." She laughed, then squirmed to get down. "I have to beat Sammy back up the hill." She said laughing as she ran. Trac looked after her wondering if he'd ever have time to raise a family. Probably not.

After a few minutes he spotted Louisa sitting under a tree chattering to three other ladies. "Sis, you have an extra quilt on the wagon?"

She looked up and Trac noted the smile on her face. "Sure... several, just help yourself." Then she went back to her conversation. Grace lay sleeping on the blanket, her tiny bonnet covering her face against the sun. His heart smote him for a second time.

He strode to her wagon and found a quilt, quickly carrying it back to where he'd left the Denton ladies. He spread it and waited while the ladies seated themselves and then joined them, keeping his booted feet over the edge.

"Beautiful day." Miss Denton sighed and lifted her face to the sun, her eyes closed.

"Tis that." Her mother agreed. "Mr. Cordera, I believe my husband mentioned you were thinking of bringing in a new herd of cattle."

Trac listened but did not give a direct answer. "Some day, Mrs. Denton."

"Now mother, you know father wouldn't like it if he knew you were talking business on such a nice day."

Trac wondered just how much the family knew about his business at the bank. Mr. Denton was well-known for his straightforwardness when it came to making money. Surely he wasn't the type to marry off his daughter to the highest bidder?

Then again . . .

He removed his hat and set it on his raised knee and stared out over the horizon, never tiring of the beauty he saw every day. He wondered how Janie was faring.

Chapter 16

I t did not take long before word came back to him through his cook. The next morning in fact.

"Hear tell you and Miz Denton had quite the time." Wes winked and then walked away quick.

"Get back here, Wes." Trac demanded, but all he heard was extra loud banging of pots in the kitchen. He smiled in spite of his gruff comment and followed Wes to the kitchen. "All right so what are the ladies saying about it?" as he grabbed a cup and poured in steaming coffee.

"Now, you ain't one for gossipin' am I right on that?"

"What's your point, Wes?"

"Hear tell, that Mr. Denton has his eyes on you for a son-in-law. That's what I heerd."

"What?" Trac turned, leaned against the wooden sink, waiting.

"You want I should repeat that?" Wes shrunk away, busying himself.

"You know what I mean. Who said that? I'd like to know."

"Now you don't get your rattles all going off and set to strike. You know how women are. Say one thing, mean another." Wes did his best to soothe his boss' irritation.

"When they say it, it's like the law around here. I already told Miss Denton I was going to be too busy to do any courting." Trac snapped his cup on the table. "What more do women need to know to understand that?"

"Nah, nah, don't get so riled up. They's all just wonderin' if ye're gonna get hitched one o'these days."

"Oh you mean like you?" Trac shot back.

"There ya go, puttin' it on me. Lookee at ya. You being young, strappin', good lookin' and still not hitched. Not to mention ya own one of the biggest ranches this side of Helena."

Trac gave his back to Wes and grabbed for a second cup of coffee. "Think that's all women think about?" He turned back.

Wes gave him a look over the top of his large nose. Trac saw his mustache tremble as though he wanted to laugh.

"You still hangin' onto your mama's skirts. You don't know women no better than that?" Wes walked out into the lean-to and brought back an apronful of potatoes and started peeling them.

"Well, if you know so much, why don't you tell me?" Wes' comment had fired him up.

"Go on with ya. I got work to do here and ye're just holdin' me up. Ain't you got nothin' to do what with all that business you gotta take care of?" Wes didn't look up.

Trac waited a few moments. "You don't know any more about women than I do." He said and snapped his Stetson on his knee and quit the kitchen. He heard a potato hit the wall behind him.

Still he hated the fact that folks were talking about Miss Denton. He didn't want to hurt her and was now in position to do just that. He returned to his office and finished up the paperwork for the day and headed up to Louisa's just as the sun was setting behind the butte.

"Wasn't that picnic just the thing?" she said smiling when he came through the door.

"Sure was." He agreed noting his sister's high color and voice full of joy.

"Mrs. Bern finally shared her pickle relish recipe after keeping it a secret for more than twenty years. She said she was too old to keep it from the young girls and gave it to us. You know she won 1st place at every fair with that recipe." Louisa turned. "Sit down, I'll get some pie."

"Sounds good, sis, but I'm plenty full. Wes cooked up a good supper tonight. Seems Mrs. Preston gave him the recipe, too."

"No!" Louisa shouted with laughter. "Well, what do you know..." she left that hanging, but Trac could see her mind working.

"Girls asleep?"

"All but Grace. She's laying on my bed, playing with mother's quilt. She just loves that old thing."

Trac lifted himself and peeked into Louisa's room. Chubby Grace lay there holding a corner of the quilt just staring at it, then putting it in her mouth and out again. When Trac moved again she saw him and her blue eyes lit up instantly and she smiled.

"Hey there little bit what's up with you?" he sat on the bed and tickled her chin, wet from slobber, then picked her up, when she raised her arms for him. "Come here to Uncle Trac." He patted her bottom and kissed the top of her fuzzy red head. "You're a handful. Been eatin' too many oats?" He rubbed the tiny back and felt her wiggle. "Ticklish, hey?" He brought her out and set her on his leg and laid his ankle across one knee, trapping her there.

"She sure is growing isn't she, Trac?" Louisa sounded faraway. "I want Emmett to see her before she's a year." She said wistfully.

"He'll be back before you know it." Trac comforted his sister, then changed the topic. "Talked to Janie?"

When Louisa hesitated he questioned her, "Something up?"

"No, not really. It's just that the girls and I went over earlier today. I tried to get Janie to let me sew her up a new dress but she refused. Said she didn't need a new dress. I pleaded with her to let me sew with her . . . like old times . . . but she just said something I didn't understand."

Trac waited quietly.

"She said, 'I'm not like you Louisa. I never will be, so stop trying to make me into you.'" Louisa turned to her brother. "Do you think I do that?" Trac read his sister's sincerity.

"I have never seen you be anything but a good friend to her, Louisa. She's not thinking straight, that's all. Probably jealous you have Emmett."

"I truly didn't think of that, Trac." She sat down. Grace leaned toward her mother and Louisa took her.

"What else can I do if every time she sees me she's jealous... and Emmett isn't even here."

"Jealousy works that way, sis. She knows Emmett's coming back to you and Billy will never be back. You can't control someone else's hurt or jealousy. I've learned that." He stood, put on his hat. "Good night, Grace, sis." He patted Grace's head and quit the cabin, leaving Louisa to her thoughts.

"Good night." He heard as the door closed behind him.

Chapter 17

"**B**oss, would ya look at this?" Wes' arm swung in an arc as he noted the sky. "'Bout as nice a day as a man could want this time o'year."

Trac dismounted and curried his horse. "What're you doing down at the barn?"

"Aw, just thought I'd come on down and help muck out them stalls...seein's as you and the boys been out all night."

"Thanks, but I'm thinkin' the boys're going to need something hefty to eat. We didn't plan on taking so long and some of them missed supper over the campfire last night. Food was gone by the time they got in. We thought they must have come on back here."

"Nope, nobody showed up. Fact is I had supper waiting."

"Yeah, we thought about that, Wes, and if we could've been here, we darn well would have. Bunch of cattle from O'H Ranch ended up in our herd."

"You don't say?" Wes' eyes narrowed.

"We drove 'em on back first thing after we knew they were among ours." Trac pushed his hat back off his sweaty brow and snapped the dust off his shirt sleeves. "Took all night, but we got 'em back."

"Good thing, I'm a thinkin'." Wes' beefy hand scratched at his chin. "Don't need no cattle thievin' talk. Ain't good...ain't good a'tall. That O'Hearn kid come a snoopin' round here some time back, 'member?"

"I remember." Trac agreed as he tossed his saddle over the stable wall in the barn. "We're going to have one bunch of hungry men in about an hour." He switched topics.

"Yep, I'm headin' up to the bunkhouse now. Got plenty left from last night, but I'd best git it ready, afore them guys bite my head off."

"Get some water heated too. I'm hankering for a warm bath."

"Yessirree boss." And Wes' was off on his bowed legs, walking with a spry step these days.

Trac noticed that he didn't hang around on Saturdays complaining no one was around to cook for.

Women.

Suddenly Trac slapped his gloved hand on the post. He'd forgotten to cut wood for Janie. The men would be back soon and he could assign the job, but that would take hours. Besides it was his job. His muscles ached as he reached for the saddle and placed it back on Job. "Looks like we got a job to do before that bath."

He let Job saunter since they'd ridden hard for the last day and most of the night. His burning eyes sought some life at the ranch. Seeing nothing, he knocked at Janie's door and waited, knowing that if she saw it was him she'd ignore it. Tired, he tied Job to a low hanging branch under the shade of a tree and picked up the ax, right where he'd left it before, stuck in a huge trunk, and began to chop.

The sun was warm, so he tossed off his shirt and worked until his back glistened with sweat. Finally finished, he stored the wood in the box on her wraparound porch and noted that very little had been used. Angry, he knocked at the door and hollered, "Janie, you in there?"

She opened and he found himself staring down the barrel of a shotgun.

"Get off my property."

Without a word he pushed the door open with his booted foot and stalked up to within two feet of her. "Shoot me. Then you could be a murderer like me." He said smoothly.

"Get out. You killed Billy as sure as if you'd shot him yourself." She shouted.

Trac eyed her straight on. "Go ahead Janie. Shoot me." His voice dangerously low.

Before Janie knew what happened, Trac grabbed the shaft of the gun and pulled it easily out of her hands. She came at him fists beating about his face. He tossed the gun, grabbed her wrists and shook her slightly.

Janie's dark eyes locked with his.

"Get hold of yourself, Janie. Now."

Instantly at the rough sound of his voice and his black eyes boring into hers, she stopped flailing. She disengaged herself from his hold and nearly lost her balance. Trac did not try to catch her. She fell to her bottom and looked at him seething with rage. "I hate you." She ground out between her teeth.

"That, I know." He turned on his heel and called over his shoulder, "Take a bath. You stink worse than a dead horse."

He could feel dirt clogs hitting his back. She had some spit left then. He smiled, mounted Job and with a glance, galloped away, leaving her sitting in the dirt. Blue, her faithful dog sitting beside her.

Chapter 18

Two weeks passed with no word from Janie. Louisa had been busy putting up the last of the late summer vegetables. All the ladies were getting ready for the long Montana winters.

"Trac, would you mind checking on Janie today?" Louisa asked when her brother came through the door. "She'll be needing her wood supply built up, but I know you've already thought of that."

"Last time I went hardly any was used." Trac grabbed a cup and dipped water from the bucket and Louisa heard the door shut quietly.

Trac hitched up and loaded half a wagonload of wood and Stetson pulled down against the wind, started out, realizing he should have grabbed a biscuit or two to eat on the way.

He didn't see Janie around so pulled up front of the ranch house and made a neat pile close to the door on the covered porch where she could get to it. The snow would be so deep she'd barely be able to keep her wits about her in the cabin alone when it really got bad. But she wouldn't listen to reason. As he unloaded and stacked, he knew there was going to be trouble. All finished, and he'd not set eyes on her. He glanced over the range, then knocked at her door. It swung open of its own accord.

"Janie." He called, fearing he may find her dead in her bed, the way she moped around, but she wasn't in the cabin.

Taking a deep breath he went back outside and scanned the countryside again. This time he saw a bit of movement near the long straight row of cottonwood trees. Stopping for a moment he went back in the house and cleaned his hands and face in the wash bowl and smoothed his wet fingers through his hair, then walked the distance.

Getting closer he could see her standing on a small hill overlooking the valley below. The wind blew her skirts and her hair was in strings. She did not turn, the wind whistling in her ears. Trac watched as she raised her hands and covered her eyes. Then she turned sideways and he stared.

A small pooch stuck out from her belly. She was with child. The wind held her dress tight to her small frame and it was apparent. Trac nearly dropped to his knees. Billy's child.

He turned on his heel and headed back for the wagon sorely needing time to think. His mind worked and worked. She was expecting a child, it was plain to see. And she had not taken care of herself. He slapped the reins and slowly turned the wagon, and headed through the field road.

At least she would have Billy's child. Surely that would or should make her happy beyond words shouldn't it? Selfishly he fought feelings of jealousy. Now she would forever be attached to Billy. She would never . . . never what? he asked himself. Love you? It would never happen. Emotions played across his face. Sorrow, sadness, a feeling of helplessness circled in his mind like a starving vulture.

He could offer to marry her in Billy's place, but she'd no more let him touch her, let alone become his wife. She would find another but it would never be him, especially now. One thing was for sure, she couldn't be alone anymore. He would see to it.

He slapped his hat against his thigh and sighed aloud, wondering if Louisa knew.

Lassoing his pride and replacing his heart with a stone, he headed back to the bunkhouse to be alone. As Providence would have it, three interruptions at the office and a visit from Louisa proved to be his undoing.

At the last he blurted out to Louisa after making small talk. "Janie's with child."

"What? She couldn't be. She would have told me. I would have seen . . ."

"I know what pregnant females look like Louisa."

Louisa colored slightly. "Of course you do." She whispered. "I just mean—" Realization set in. "Oh Trac, Billy's child. Do you think that will help her in her grief? How like the Lord to give her a blessing in spite of everything." She breathed out, "Oh Lord, thank you."

Trac stared at his sister. She had a fine heart. She thought only of Janie's good, whereas he thought about his own loss. The promise he'd made to himself to harden his heart had not worked, as though wishing he didn't love Janie would make it so. Thus far he'd been like flint and had never let anyone know. Even Louisa, for he'd never let on, preferring to let sleeping dogs lie.

Now things were different.

Chapter 19

The first week of October arrived with sunshine and many tasks yet to finish. Trac met with his men at dawn on the first Monday to set up the week's list of chores. "Tan, you and Riley come with me today. We'll gather up the strays and get the south fences mended. Once the snow sets in it'll be a long time before we see the ground again. Tom, you, Dan and Cash can get the barn cleaned out, put new straw in the stalls, and repair the damage done by the last storm. We'll have Wes pack us a meal and the rest can eat at the bunkhouse as usual. Don't expect us until late; maybe not until tomorrow if things are worse than I expect. Any questions."

"Yeah, Boss, what about Billy's place? Crew's down to three men. Two more up and quit yesterday."

Trac hadn't heard that. He'd been so busy he hadn't heard.

"She cain't stay there during the winter. We're going to be short-handed as it is." Dan finished.

Trac heard his men murmuring.

"Cain't you get her to stay the winter with her ma?" One suggested.

"She's all yours if you want to try." Trac sighed.

Several of the men shook their heads

Trac turned and placed his Stetson firmly on his head and headed for the door, his chaps flapping, boots clicking on the old wood floor. *Wouldn't be long before everyone knew about Janie's child anyway.* And he knew one thing. Janie would *not* be staying alone at the ranch.

"He sure don't seem to care much what happens to Janie," One said quietly. "Not like him."

Tan spoke up. "Trac and me's been over to Janie's place nearly half this summer trying to get her set for winter." He turned and walked away. Ranch hands hardly said two words, but when they did they were important.

"That he has, 'cause I been helpin' myself," Riley added. "That's why we were late in getting' things done around here."

The men, slowly, but purposely headed for their duties and no more was said.

Cash, Dan, and Tom headed down to the barn Trac, Tan, and Riley set off west.

"Don't worry boss, they'll see to Billy's place all right, but sure is a shame Janie won't go to her ma's. She'd be better off an all. That'll only set you to havin' to watch out for her and if this year's bad, ain't gonna be no picnic."

Trac said nothing but appreciated Riley's thought.

The three men kicked in their heels and no more talk was necessary. Work on the range was hard, long, and rough. Trac appreciated the loyalty of his men and discovered time and again how much work they did and without complaint.

Surveying the damage from the recent storm the men found a huge tree toppled over at the roots and several branches lying about. "Looks like a big wind took this 'un down." Dan dropped out of his saddle. "Yep, thing is it took down a good chunk o'fencing too. Look yonder. Could be where those cattle been takin' off to."

"Let's get that taken care of today boys. We got enough wire?"

"Looks like it boss. We can do most of it anyway."

They set to work and did not stop until time for supper. "Good thing Wes packed up some vittles . . . we're not going to get home tonight." Tan spoke up.

"Right." Trac agreed. "Okay boys, let's eat and finish up here for the night."

His style was easy and his men appreciated that. Some ranch owners thought themselves above the law and mankind, but not Trac.

The three ate in silence, contemplating tomorrow's work. When all was packed away and they lay on the ground under a patch of trees, Tan spoke. "Trac, any chance you could buy Billy's farm?" He asked hesitantly.

Trac lay with his hands behind his head gazing up at the stars poking holes in the wide black, expansive sky. "Don't think Janie'll sell."

Tan and Riley exchanged looks across the campfire but said nothing. Janie would never be able to keep up that ranch and both men knew Trac would work himself to death to make up for that bet he made with Billy.

Two days passed, food and wire had run out. At the end of the third day the men picked up their camping gear and rode out. They would have to come back tomorrow.

"Trac you look beat. Riley and I could finish up here, if you'd send back some vittles, we could finish the job." Tan suggested.

"Yeah, boss no problem." Riley agreed.

"Thanks, but I'd rather be working."

The men shrugged. A man could kill himself for sure running two big ranches. But he was the boss.

Suddenly the winds picked up and a powerful icy rain storm blew in. Trac picked up his pace, stopping long enough to pull out his slicker and drag it over his body. He tried not to think about Janie there in the cabin, in her condition, but it was impossible. She carried a child now and he could not let her spend the winter in the cabin alone. No one, not even her ma, could talk any sense into her. It had been months since Billy's death and Janie had not left her bed of grief.

If it had to be done he'd carry her bodily kicking and screaming to her mother's, deposit her there, then come back and lock up her place and nail the doors and windows shut. *Doubtful she'll really care where she's at anyway,* he thought.

Prayers went up for what he was about to do. Trac had seen the handiwork of God out in this glorious and dangerous land and knew that God cared about man. *Lord you know all things and I gotta tell ya things aren't lookin' too good right now. Billy's dead, Janie's alone and now there's a child coming. I'm the only one to look after her and she hates the sight of me – not to mention the fact that I've got my heart all wrapped up in her.* The icy rain pelted down as the three rode in a wide line.

You know I can't take care of Billy's place with Janie there, Lord. I know she wants to be close to Billy, but I can't be worryin' about her all the time. I got Louisa and the girls to look after, not to mention Janie's mother. All these women. I'm only one man, Lord.

For Trac, praying had always been a way to send his trouble upward to Someone who knew all. Somehow he felt better and relaxed his aching back against the saddle once again.

The Bible verses he had learned at his mother's knee had served him well. "Casting all your care upon him, for He careth for you." Came to mind.

Back at the ranch the hands had returned for the night and were sitting down to supper.

"Smells awful good in here." Trac yelled as he opened the door wide, stomping his muddy boots at the door, eager to hear how things had gone. "The men are unloading the wagon and they'll be up here quick." He spoke to Wes.

"We were startin' to wonder if'n we ought to come looking for ya." Tom laughed, snapping his hat in the air. "But since they were with the boss, we figured, you was working 'em to death!"

Everyone laughed and Trac took it all in good-naturedly, glad to be back at the table with his men. "Bosses ain't God." He threw back and finished washing up. He sat down with his men to eat, the smell of sweaty bodies filling the old bunkhouse, but no one seemed to notice.

"I'm headin' out for a bath." He said quietly as everyone was pushing away from the table. Everyone looked up at once, Tom asking the obvious, "In this weather?"

"Yep. Rain or no rain, I need a bath. Some of you do, too." He grabbed some clean clothes from his bunkroom and slammed the door behind him. They all shrugged. They were not going to bathe in the cold rain, smell or no.

What he really wanted was to feel something. He stomped to the creek a few hundred yards away, stripped away his dirty clothes, and walked quickly into the water. He dropped down as a sharp intake of breath swooshed from this throat.

Teeth chattering, he soaped up and made short work of a bath. Water sluicing over his body, he quickly stepped into clean clothes and immediately became wet again from the light rain. He hurried toward Louisa's cabin...needing to see how things were going and sit by a warm fire.

After two knocks, Louisa, already in her night clothes and a wrapper, greeted him with a whisper.

"Come in. We were worried about you." She stepped up on her tiptoes and gave him a kiss on the cheek. "You're soaked through. Where have you been?" Her hands were resting at her hipbones again. "You smell good."

"Took a bath." He smiled still shivering.

"Well, for goodness' sake Trac, you could have chosen another day." Louisa scolded. "At the very least it would have been prudent to use your washtub. Here, let me take your shirt and dry it by the fire. We'll have time for talking. The girls are already asleep."

"That's what I came for...and to check up on you and girls. Any word from Emmett?"

"Got a letter this morning. Tom went in for the mail and a few supplies."

"What's up, you smiling and all?"

"Oh nothing. I should be crying, but Emmett did find another nugget. A big one." She laughed hanging his shirt across a twig chair.

"Yeah? How big?"

"Should get at least a thousand dollars for it." She exclaimed, clapping her small hands together.

"What? That's a fortune. Does that mean he's headed home to build that house up on the hill for you?"

"No." Her voice lowered. "It only means he'll be gone longer."

Trac knew why immediately. Once a man got a taste of riches, he could never stop. It went that way for most of them.

"Guess you'll need to talk some sense into him, Trac. I love him so much, but I want him home . . . it doesn't matter that we're not rich. I have everything here I could ever want."

Trac stared at the fire as he heard his sister's voice float off into the distance.

"I know we need a place of our own, so you can have ma and pa's place back but . . ."

"Whoa, hold on. Who said I wanted the place back?"

"Well, you worked the land and pa gave you the deed. And you haven't charged us a nickel."

"You and Emmett and the girls can stay as long as you want. If I want a cabin, I'll build one. Is that clear?"

"Well, yes, but one day you'll marry and..."

Trac interrupted. "Don't count on it. I've got other plans."

Louisa turned and looked at his profile, for he was staring at the fire. She clamped her lips together.

Minutes passed as the fire crackled in the small room.

"Everything okay, Trac?"

"Fine." He stopped her before she got him talking too much. He had to keep his feelings about Janie to himself.

"Is it Janie?" She asked.

He saw her tip her head sideways, trying to read his mind. His chair scraped across the floor as he stood. "How is Janie?" he asked turning the tables and his back to warm his backside.

"She's fine. I visited her yesterday while you were gone. "She *is* with child." She sighed.

Trac stared into the fire. He knew that.

"So did you talk to her about moving back with her mother?"

"I did but you know Janie. She's hardly eating anything, Trac. I'm worried for her and the child."

"Would she come and spend the winter with you and the girls? That would be sensible. You'd have company and could watch out for her. She could help you, too."

"Janie's not one to be sensible." She said and Trac knew she was right.

"Does that mean she plans on staying there all winter?" He rubbed his hands together standing nearer the fire.

"So she says."

"She won't be staying."

Louisa looked up but thought it best to keep her tongue. Trac was just as stubborn as Janie was and far be it from her to say so. "Sit down in the rocker, Trac and rest. You look tired. You could use some shut-eye while your shirt dries."

Trac settled his big frame into her rocker and crossed his ankles far out in front of him, laid his head back and closed his eyes.

She had to step over his booted feet each time she passed, but it was good to see him relaxing. He worked too hard. And carried a burden he couldn't toss off. With her and the girls and now Janie's place to look after, he was going to work himself to death. And then what would they all do.

Louisa snatched the baby's clothing drying over a small wooden rack near the fire and scolded herself for worrying. She folded each piece and stacked the tiny garments on the table, every now and again gazing at her brother. Once when she passed, she reached out and smoothed a stubborn lock of wet hair into place. He was a fine man.

After a time Trac awoke with a start. He had been dreaming about Janie. She had fallen into the creek and he hadn't been able to find her in the rushing waters. Breathing hard, he came to himself and realized he was still at Louisa's. She had fallen asleep sitting at the table, her head resting on her arms.

"Louisa." He gently prodded her.

She looked up sleepy-eyed. "I must have fallen asleep." And yawned.

"Yep, get yourself to bed. Let the latch down after I leave."

Louisa stood wearily and after the latch was safely in place, made her way to her bed.

Chapter 20

The days passed quickly. The icy rain had snatched the autumn leaves off the branches and left them laying thick on the ground. Trac spent more time on the back of his horse than anywhere the last two weeks. Hard work gave him a small respite from his thoughts. But at night if it was warm enough to sleep under the stars, he had put his hands beneath his head and relished the quiet all around him, while thoughts of Janie spiraled through his head.

Louisa had visited Janie more often and he stayed away, hoping his heart would harden against her. Janie would be better off with someone else, he reasoned. She could never care for him, but he still felt the sting of hatred, and worse, disappointment each time she looked at him.

Through Louisa, just last night, he had learned that Janie's mother had tried in vain to get her stubborn daughter to return home, especially now that she knew she was with child. Janie had alienated everyone except Louisa and even Louisa had learned to keep her distance at times, hoping Janie would see the error of her ways.

* * *

The first week of December was deceitfully warmer than usual for this time of year. Things at the ranch had slowed a bit. Trac knew he could not avoid Janie forever and had been away long enough that he'd actually stopped thinking of her so often.

After the noon meal, he'd given the guys the day off so they could make a last-minute run to town for their winter supplies. Louisa was too busy taking advantage of the weather, washing and hanging her bed sheets and blankets to be bothered with visiting.

"I've been granted another day." She told Trac, "And I'm going to use it. Isn't it just beautiful today? The sky is blue, the clouds are white as cotton balls." She hadn't even noticed that Trac had left.

At first sight of Janie's place, Trac had seen movement. A bit of brown calico that she seemed to wear more often than not these days, whipped in the soft wind. She was sweeping the leaves from the big porch he and Billy had built.

They'd been so proud of the workmanship; the fancy hand-turned railing, the extra wide steps. They'd patted each other on the back while Janie brought them lemonade. It had been finished only weeks after their wedding trip. Billy had wanted it done when Janie returned from her ma's. She'd had to run off for nearly ten days after her ma took sick. She hated leaving Billy. Trac remembered the day.

She had stepped out of the cabin and waited for Billy to come to her. "I wish you could come with me Billy. I'll be so lonely without you and us just married." She had smiled through her tears. "I hate to leave you so soon."

"Honey, I got something I got to do here, but me and Trac'll stop by next week, all right?" Billy had smoothed her hair and she had acquiesced. Billy loved Janie like he loved his horse. Trac had turned away to stare out at the Montana sky that day to avoid witnessing Billy's gentle ministrations to his new wife.

It was at that point Trac remembered thinking about getting himself a wife. If he could be half as fortunate to find someone like Janie, he thought to try.

Now she was here and there was no chance this side of a miracle he'd ever be able to tell her how he felt. He nudged Job forward. Janie had looked up but showed no emotion. She kept on sweeping and if Trac didn't know better, her sweeps had become more violent the minute she knew it was him.

"Beautiful day." He stated cordially, dropping to the ground. He slapped his hat against his thigh out of pure habit, releasing the dust into the wind and walked slowly toward her, but kept his distance.

She kept up her vicious movements, purposely turning her back to him. He stared out at the western sky. "Need anything done around here?" He asked without moving.

"No. Least of all from you." Her voice wavered.

Silence hovered around like a sky full of vultures and finally Trac let loose. He'd had enough. Stalking up to her he took the broom from her hand. She fought him but he won easily. "Sit down." He ordered, pointing to the one rocking chair on the porch.

She stomped to the chair and sat, her arms crossed over her chest.

"It's clear to see you're . . . you're, with child." He uttered, feeling foolish.

"So?"

"So what're you doing out here swinging that broom as though there were no tomorrow?"

"None of your business. Now get off my land."

"Not until I'm done saying my piece. You're gonna listen this time, woman." He set the broom against the house and immediately the wind tossed it down and it slammed to the wood planks, echoing eerily.

She stood and made a move toward the door. Trac grabbed her arm and gently but firmly pulled her back. She yanked her elbow from his hold and glared.

"Don't touch me."

"Don't worry, I won't if you'll stand still."

"Say what you have to say, then leave."

"You are the most selfish, bitter woman in these here parts."

She cocked her head and her look said, "So."

"There's a child to be thought of and you look like a ghost, all skin and bones."

She continued to stare, but he went on. "You can't stay here in the cabin through the winter, you ... being with child. Go in and pack your things because I'm taking you to your ma's."

He hadn't meant to put it quite as harshly; it was obvious to any thick-headed person that that was the only way this stubborn woman was going to do anything.

"I'm staying here and you can't make me do anything – least of all make me leave Billy's home." She was standing now.

"I can and I will." Trac was sick to death of her willfulness and made a move toward her.

Her eyes filled with tears and she stomped her foot. "I will not leave here. It means nothing to you, but I loved Billy and I'm not leaving our home, baby or no baby."

Trac turned from her to keep from pulling her into his arms and holding her until she died to her pain. He garnered his strength and turned back to face her.

"Janie, you know that you'll be putting your life into danger and the child's too, with no one out here to help you. How do you expect to give birth without any help?"

"I can manage. I've managed everything else, including losing my beloved husband." She reminded him with a shaky voice. "Besides Louisa has done this before…"

He stayed quiet for a time, his hands shoved into his back pockets. "No Janie, you can't manage. That's just it. We've all been as patient as we can be; your ma, Louisa and me. Even my ranch hands know you're doing the wrong thing. They got more sense than you." Immediately he regretted that last sentence.

"Sense? You talk about sense? What sense did it make that God should take my husband? I wish . . ." she couldn't go on.

He knew what she meant to say.

"Why don't you just say it, Janie? You wish it would've been me and not Billy who died that day."

Her face turned bright red and she burst out with an intense bitterness that set Trac back a step. "All right, I'll say it. I wish it had been you. You didn't have someone who loved you like your own life. I wish Billy would have lived and you would have died."

She ran from him and he didn't stop her.

He heard the door slam behind him. How little she knew about his heart. He did love someone. He wondered if it hurt more to lose someone you loved through death knowing you could never see them again, or if it hurt more to love someone you see every day but could never have.

Hurt flushed out his well-meaning task and he slowly walked back to his horse. What else could he do?

Suddenly he stopped short. What else indeed! He turned on his heel, mind made up, stomped into the cabin, the door slamming hard against the wall and said, "Get your things. We're leaving now."

She didn't move from her face-down position on the bedstead and he raised his voice, "Get your things or leave without 'em."

She continued to cry into her arms and he no longer felt sorry for her. She wasn't capable of making a decent decision these days and by God's grace he was going to do it for her.

He reached down and picked her up off the bed and set her on her feet.

"Get out of here you . . . you. . ."

"Say what you will Janie, but you're leaving, with or without your things. You've got ten minutes to pack."

He walked out the door and having no place to go, knowing she might try to hide from him, he took a seat on the front porch stoop and waited. No sound came from the cabin. What would he do if she refused to pack? Lift her over his shoulder and carry her off? He would have done just that, but the child inside her prevented him from doing such a thing. So now he faced a dilemma.

He waited a full ten minutes and went back in. Janie sat in her rocker, tipping back and forth incessantly, her small feet touching the floor with each tip. The look on her face and the hold she had on the rocker arms told him she was not moving.

"Look Janie. I know you loved Billy, but he wouldn't have wanted you to do this, especially now with a child coming."

She said nothing, her facial features seemed to harden even more. The beautiful woman he knew now looked spiteful and uncomely.

Finally she spoke through gritted teeth. "If you take me anywhere, I'll come right back."

And he knew she meant it.

"You are not the girl I used to know." He said quietly and turned to leave.

She jumped up in a rage and grabbed the back of his leather vest, jerking him backward.

"I'm not a girl and I am not the same woman. I have died. Do you realize what I'm saying?" She shouted louder. "I have died inside. Not you or anyone else is going to change me. Can't you get that through your head?"

She released her hold and Trac looked down into her small face. Her brown eyes had lost their life, their luster, her hair was tangled and dirty. She looked twenty years older than her nineteen years.

Trac faced her squarely. "You used to be so bright, so full of life, so fun."

"And what changed that?" She responded bitterly.

"It was God Janie. I didn't call Billy home. God did." He spun and started to walk away, but she stopped him with her words.

"No, you just helped him along."

For the first time in his life, he wished to strike a woman. Shocked, he turned back, took the top of her arms into his grasp and pulled her face up to his and spit out, "You are a miserable woman, Janie Cordera."

He let her go and she toppled a bit from the quick movement, but gained her footing. She, for the first time, had been shocked into silence.

He couldn't get away from her quick enough. A fast gallop sent him flying into the afternoon sun, glad he got away without injuring her person. He had nearly lost his mind at her continuous accusations and was tired to death of them.

It would be a long time before he approached her again. God was asking too much. He headed back to the bunkhouse where he could be alone. Wes and the guys had all gone to Helena and wouldn't be back for three days. He wrote a quick note and slapped it over the nail by the door, then packed some vittles in a saddle bag, threw on his bedroll and took off west. Sleeping under the stars would give him time to think.

Chapter 21

Two days and nights under the stars proved to be a blessed time. He'd grabbed his mother's Bible on the way out the door at the last moment and read during daylight hours. Passages kept coming to him until he had finally calmed down and felt like he could reason again.

When asked how many times a man had to forgive, Jesus had said, "Seventy times seven." That being an awful lot, Trac knew in order to have peace in his own mind, he had to forgive Janie. But how do you forgive someone who won't let you? He wondered time and again.

Finally the answer came. She would never forgive him. But he had to forgive her. Somehow he would and asked for God's help, for he had nothing in his own soul that wished to do so.

A week later he felt strong enough to try again. This time it was early morning. He'd talked to Louisa and she'd promised to pray and had sent along fresh baked bread and a tiny white gown that she'd sewn for the baby, hoping it would encourage Janie to think of the child.

"Good morning, Janie."

She looked up with a startled expression.

"Didn't you hear me coming?"

"No." She stopped working and leaned on the broom. She'd been sweeping snow off the porch.

"You look tired. Louisa sent some bread and this." He held out the tiny gown.

Janie saw it dangling from his tan work-worn big hand and flew inside.

Trac would not be put off.

He stepped inside the cabin, placed the bread on the table. The place was untidy. She was sitting in the rocker, tipping back and forth, her face expressionless.

"Don't you want the gown for the babe?" his voice was tender.

"No. I'm not going to keep it." She announced firmly.

"I see." Trac answered wisely. "Well, I'll just put it here and you can save it for whoever raises Billy's child."

She stared at him, bitterness eating at her once-lovely face.

He turned to leave and noticed she followed. He mounted Job and saw her out of the corner of his eye. She'd picked up the broom and was brushing the snow aside with a vengeance, while the wind just scattered it back again. He let her be and rode off slowly.

Then a clunking sound tore through the wind and echoed toward him. He looked back warily and saw that Janie had dropped to the porch in a heap. The broom handle had hit the wood soundly, alerting him. He was at her side in a moment, scooping her up. She was light as a newborn pup.

Gently he laid her on her bed and looked down at her. Her face was flushed. A cool cloth would take care of that. He laid it across her forehead and pushed her hair away from her face. She felt hot.

After a while she came around. Trac held her hand, rubbing her arm, trying to pull her back into consciousness. She opened her eyes and shut them again. In a few moments she began to focus. She jerked her arm from his hand and gave him her back.

He left her alone, thinking it best not to upset her and went out and made himself busy in the yard. First thing he swept the remainder of the snow from the porch and brought more wood inside. Then he went down to the barn and fed and watered the animals.

He knocked once and stepped inside. Clearly she was surprised to see he was still there. She was on her feet.

"Looks like Milly is going to be calving soon. You'd best watch her and call me when it's near her time."

She stared at him, pushed her hair out of her eyes and continued straightening the room. He washed his face in the bowl and poured a tin full of water with the spoon. "Have you eaten today?"

"No. I forgot. That's why I was light-headed. Nothing wrong otherwise."

"I see. I could sure use some lunch." He hinted at her back.

She stiffened but set a plate of bread on the table. "Tell Louisa thanks for the bread.

"Got any coffee?"

"Haven't made any in quite a while. Billy was the only one to drink it."

"I know you like tea. Have you any left?"

"Yes."

"Mind if I have a cup...sugar please."

"You don't have to be so polite."

Trac noticed she never used his name anymore. God forgive him, he'd always liked to hear his name on her lips. He had not heard it once since Billy died.

She set the tea on the table and sat down herself, sipped the tea with shaking hands, and barely touched the bread.

"You have to eat."

She ignored him.

When they finished the silent meal he stood. "Pack up some things. I'm taking you to your ma's place."

"No. I already told you . . ."

She stopped when he stood and came toward her. "I can pick you up and take you with the clothes on your back or you can take a minute and grab some things. Which will it be?"

His eyes never left hers. He was not shouting. Just stating the facts.

She looked wary.

He stood firm. "Well?"

With spit in her eye, she turned and headed for her room and was back in a minute with a dress rolled up, looking for all the world like a little girl who was running away from home.

"Is that all you're taking?" He looked down at the small bundle.

She colored when she saw her unmentionables hanging out. Stuffing them back into the dress, she turned to save face and he smiled.

"You'll need those, too."

Her reddened face gave her away, but she said nothing.

"It's the only dress I've let out at the seams to accommodate my . . . my . . ." she finished lamely.

"Your waistline." He finished smiling down at her. "When is the young one due?"

She hesitated. "Near as I can figure, sometime in late February

"Right in Montana's worst blizzard time. It's good you're going to your mother's Janie."

Tired of the friendly talk, she reverted back. "Let's go. I'm tired and you're boring me to death with your concern." She shrugged into her coat.

"I'll go down and get your wagon." The door closed behind him softly.

Whistling as he went he felt a powerful calmness about the situation. At least she was going to her mother's. Finally.

Setting the blankets upon the hard seat for her; he'd folded them double so she wouldn't be bounced around too much, especially now. He reined in Billy's favorite old mare, then sat quietly on the porch looking over the grand landscape, which would soon be covered in four foot-high snow drifts.

Trac jumped down to help her up, but she insisted she could make it herself. He waited but didn't touch her even when she struggled to pull herself up. She settled on the blankets as far away from him as she could. He smiled but said nothing. She looked off and away from him.

They rode in silence for awhile. "It's beautiful this time of year isn't it?"

She barely grumbled at him but he didn't mind at all.

An hour later they were at Janie's ma's. He'd taken great care to go slow even after she'd urged him to hurry on. The older woman came running out to greet her daughter.

"Have you come to stay?" she inquired anxiously.

"For awhile, Mother, but I'm going back as soon as I can manage."

"Of course you will. Just come inside. We've much to talk about."

Trac caught Janie's eyes and for a moment he understood that Janie would not be happy here. Her mother was a worrier, constantly chattering about something or other and Trac knew it would be hard. For the first time, and in a single look, they'd shared an understanding.

"Won't be for long." He whispered, "and then you can get back home."

"Not soon enough." She sighed.

Trac rode away more satisfied with himself and Janie than he'd been since Billy died.

Chapter 22

S everal weeks later, Louisa came stomping down through the snow drifts to the bunkhouse. "Wes is Trac in his office?"

"Sure is honey, just go on in. He's been holed up in there for hours. Even skipped lunch."

"Oh dear. Can I take him something?"

"I'll get a cup of coffee and some sweetbread."

Louisa balanced the cup and plate together and tapped her foot on the door.

"It's me Trac."

"Come in Louisa."

She entered and Trac jumped up to help her.

"Hey, what's all this about? You tromping in the snow to come down here. Anything wrong, Sis?"

She waved off his comment. "Wes sent this in, said you hadn't stopped to eat."

"Yeah, busy. Time got away. Any news from Emmett?"

"No news, but I expect a letter any day. Little Grace has been so fussy for the past month. She's got her first tooth."

"Hey how about that." Trac smiled. "You look tired though."

"These last few nights she's hardly slept. I've tried rubbing her gums with oil of clove, but nothing seemed to help. Hopefully now that the tooth has appeared she'll settle down and sleep through the night. I could use a good night's rest."

"Hey why don't we cook up a side of beef tomorrow. Celebrate Grace's tooth and let Wes do the cooking. What do you say?"

"Oh Trac, that sounds wonderful. I'd love it. I could bake the bread, make some pudding..."

"Whoa...hold on there. The whole idea is to give you a rest. Wes' chomping at the bit to cook up something big. You know he loves to pack out a good meal."

"Of course." She smiled.

"Good. Heard anything from Janie?"

Louisa lifted the heavy oil cloth at the window and peered out to give her a moment to decide how to tell her brother the news. "Janie's gone back home, Trac."

"What?" He stood up, tipping his chair backward and the coffee cup with it.

"Oh dear, I knew you'd be upset." She sopped up the coffee off the wood floor with his handkerchief while he righted his chair.

"Right near her time? What is she thinking Louisa?" He ran his fingers through his hair.

"I know. I know. Her ma couldn't stop her."

"How'd she get there?"

"Josiah Wilson."

"Wilson? What's he doing nosing around here?"

"Seems he heard about Janie's predicament and has been visiting Janie at her mothers for some time now."

"I see." He ground out.

"Don't worry, Trac. I don't think Janie really likes him . . . she's just lonely."

Standing now to his feet, he paced the small space in his office. He knew what loneliness could do. "Why should I worry about Josiah Wilson? If she wants him, what's that to me? Just another burden off my back."

"Trac, you don't mean that." Louisa admonished him.

"Not in the way you think, Louisa. I just mean that if that's what she wants, what harm would it be? She's lonely. The child needs a father . . ."

"I know." She sighed. It's all so sad isn't it?"

Trac nodded. "I'll talk to Wes about tomorrow." and left the room.

He had to get out of the stuffiness that seemed to engulf him. Josiah Wilson with Janie. The thought made him sick.

She was so far advanced in her pregnancy, maybe he should be thankful. At least she had someone to look after her. For she certainly would not let him near.

Chapter 23

January 1885

S evere winter storms covered the wild Montana buttes and valleys while Trac struggled to keep everything going. The stock needed food and water every day and he and his men were wearing themselves out. And it was birthing season. There were already 17 new calves to feed and at last count twenty six more on the way. When Dan broke his wrist trying to wrangle a batch of longhorns into the gate, leaving them one man short, Trac knew something had to be done.

Thankfully, two of Billy's men, both single, agreed to stay on through the winter. That left him free of those duties, at least for now, and free from seeing Janie so much.

Stomping through the two feet of new snow he made his way to Louisa's on a cold January evening. A swoosh of snow followed him in and he was hit by the warmth from the hearth.

Trac, it's good to see you. Give me your coat. Have you eaten?"

"Just finished." He seated himself after rubbing his hands together at the fire. His voice brought Virginia from her bedroom.

"Snow is boring." She muttered.

"Anybody up to a game of checkers?" He shot Virginia a look.

"I am." She waved her arms.

"Why don't you two play and I'll get Grace to bed." Louisa smiled at her brother, grateful for the intercession.

"Can I sit on your lap, Uncle Trac? I miss my daddy."

"Sure, come on over here." He threw out his arms. She settled into the crook of his arm and they played another game.

After a time, she lay her head on his shoulder, then held her hand next to his ear and whispered, "I want my daddy to come home." And he saw the tears form in her soft brown eyes.

"Me, too. He'll be home before you know it. Daddy will build you a big house on the hill, remember the one I showed you?"

"Um.....hmmm...she nodded her head against his shoulder. "But I don't want to be rich. I like this house."

"Well now I don't blame you a bit. You'd rather have your daddy than a new house. While we're waiting, let's teach you a few tricks on this checker board so when daddy comes you can fool him and beat him."

"All right, Uncle Trac." She lifted her head and sat up straighter and he patiently taught her the finer skills of the game.

Louisa watched from the doorway. Trac meant everything to her. So did his happiness. He was worn out and it showed.

Once Grace was asleep, she worked while her daughter and brother played the game. She loved hearing them laugh.

"Now off to bed with you Virginia."

She jumped down with a frown.

"Hey, didn't you forget something?" Trac teased her.

She stepped up on her tippy toes and kissed his cheek. He knew few sweeter moments than the trust and love on a child's innocent face. "Now you dream lots of happy things and soon daddy'll be home."

"Okay." She yawned.

Trac looked at his sister thoughtfully. Louisa was a strong woman and yet looked like a young girl. She'd married Emmett when she was seventeen, Virginia had come along almost immediately and then a few years later, Grace.

"I'm really proud of you, sis."

"Me?" She waved the comment aside.

"Yes, you've grown up. Taking care of the girls and without Emmett here..."

"That's because you're here." She snagged him with a playful tap on the shoulder. "And speaking of which, I have been meaning to give you a good talking to."

"Oh? What about?"

"You have been working too hard, Trac. Look at you, you're at least twenty pounds lighter and your face looks strained sometimes."

"You worry too much. I'm fine."

Louisa fiddled with her knitting a bit and then looked up. "Billy's ranch is killing you."

Now he stood and went to the window, wiping the frost off the tiny windowpane in circular motion where he could look out and avoid his sister's knowing gaze. "I'm handling it. It's tough. I knew from the start it would be. But it has to be done."

"Only because Janie insists on making herself a nuisance."

"How is she anyway?" He changed the subject skillfully.

"She's fine. The child is due this month. I'm going to be needing a ride down there if the sun'll melt off some of this new snow. It's been nearly two weeks since she moved back. The only other person she sees is Josiah, and it's just not proper, him hanging around all the time with no one there."

Trac stiffened at the name. Josiah's around a lot you say?"

"Yes he is and I'm glad in one way. He can do some of the chores around Billy's place."

"He's not . . . living there is he?" Trac's voice almost gave him away.

"No, of course not." She looked surprised at the question. "He comes almost every day, though, and Janie lets him."

"If it suits her." Trac said and that was the end of it.

A few moments of silence fell upon them, Trac standing at the window, Louisa's knitting needles clicking . . . the fire crackling.

"I miss Ma and Pa at times like this."

Louisa's voice was pensive, Trac knew from too many long winter days and nights.

"Do you suppose they know how we're doing?" she asked staring into the fire.

"I believe they do. God has his ways to comfort both the ones that are with Him and those of us who've yet to go to Him."

"That's a comforting thought." She sighed.

"You're thinking of Emmett too aren't you?" He took a seat.

"Oh yes. Sometimes I miss him so terribly I can hardly stand it. I want him with me at night and coming home to supper and talking with me and the girls. He barely knows Grace – and she's grown so much."

Trac saw the need in his sister's face and wondered how a man could stay away from his family, even for gold. Shrugging, he lifted himself from the chair and a groan escaped his mouth. "Getting stiff in my old age." He laughed.

"You're much too tired, Tracson Gage Cordera, and well you know it. Now scuttle yourself to the bunkhouse and get some rest."

"Yes ma'am." He saluted.

"Trac, at the first sign of sun, plan on taking me to Janie's. She needs a woman to check on her these days. It's nearing her time."

"Yes, ma'am." he repeated, as he shrugged into his great coat.

"Now off with you." She held the door while he hurried out into the moonlit winter night. She cleaned off a window pane and watched until she could see him no more, a dark bundle leaning into the blinding wind and snow.

"What would me and the girls do without you, brother?" She sighed.

Chapter 24

Two days later the sun was blindingly bright. The snow had stopped falling and now it sparkled like a million diamonds spread over the land.

"When's Uncle Trac coming?" Virginia pleaded for the fourth time.

"Soon, listen for the horses." Her mother called out.

"We're going to spend the day with Janie sewing for the baby. Be sure you don't leave the snips behind or we'll all be cross with you."

"I won't ma."

"I think I'll take these leftover pieces of yarn, make use of them!" Louisa hustled around picking up any little scrap that could be used as a decoration.

Everything lay stacked against the wall awaiting Trac's arrival. Suddenly, the sounds of bells could be heard echoing over the heaps of snow.

"He's here, ma. And he has the sleigh!" Virginia yelled.

"I'm right here dear. No need to shout so." She peered out the window pane.

Louisa's thoughts scattered back to several years before when her father and then Emmett drove the sleigh…her heart hurt for a moment, then she remembered the delights of childhood and hurried, glad to be on a magical journey through the snow covered fields.

"Come now, let's make sure we have everything, so Uncle Trac won't have to make so many trips."

Fifteen minutes later, after much talking and hullabaloo Trac had his girls loaded up and gliding through the snow easily, up and down the hills and even across the small pond.

"Do you think it's safe?" Louisa worried.

"It's safe." Trac glanced at his sister, noting her hands gripped in her lap.

"You had better pray it is, because if anything happens...

She was interrupted by a big bump and they all laughed when Louisa cried out.

"Oh Ma, you're just a fraidy-cat like Samson." Samson was their newest barn cat and was indeed easily frightened, Louisa had to agree.

Janie had no idea she was about to be pounced upon by such a large group and Louisa reminded them that she might not feel up to a lot of noise; which after she thought about it, was too late to worry about now. Janie was getting a houseful and that was that. If Janie was tired, Louisa would see to it she napped.

"I've got a few tools to unload and I'll be down at the barn with the men while you ladies have your fun." Her brother teased.

"Oh don't worry. We won't be having all fun. There will be supper to cook for us all and we've got special things planned."

"Is that so? We'll I doubt you can surprise me." Trac's laugh resounded over the snowy slopes.

Louisa gave her brother a look.

The ride took longer than usual; but even Grace, hidden in her many wrappings, barely able to peek out, was satisfied. It was a fine Montana winter day.

When they finally pulled up, Trac saw a horse tied to the front stoop and looked at Louisa.

"Josiah Wilson." She whispered.

Trac said nothing, just sidled the sleigh up near the cabin and stepped down.

"Would you mind knocking first, Trac? Janie has no idea we're coming.

He stomped through the snow, noting her wood supply was dwindling and knocked loudly.

"Josiah." He greeted the man and offered his hand. "We're here to see Janie."

"Sorry, but she's resting." Josiah Wilson stood firm, both hands on either side of the doorway.

"Well, she has company. Louisa and the girls are here for some merriment. You know women."

"Janie doesn't need company." Josiah stated rudely and was about to shut the door when Trac heard Janie's voice from inside.

"Please invite them in, Josiah. I'm nigh unto boredom; it would do me good to visit."

Trac paid no heed to the body filling the doorway and stepped to the sleigh to carry Virginia and set her down on the porch. Louisa followed with Grace.

Josiah Wilson frowned and was pushed back against the wall.

"What in the world are all of you going to do?" he inquired stiffly, his eyes narrowing.

Trac noticed he had his boots off and was in his stocking feet. For some reason that bothered him.

Janie appeared in the doorway, thin and bent over from the heaviness of her condition. She pushed her hair back and smiled weakly. "Come in. It's so good to see you." She said to Louisa.

Trac noted she didn't acknowledge his presence. He noted her melancholy voice and her dark eyes had no shine in them. He wanted to put his fist through the pane. Instead he headed out to the barn glad for the wind in his face and something to do with his hands.

"Josiah would you mind stepping back so I can pick up the things behind you?" Louisa asked politely, reaching around to snatch Janie's still damp clothing off the makeshift line running across the back of the room. She lay each piece across Janie's bed to finish drying and out of sight.

"There, that will make a bit more room. Now we'll move the table nearer the window where the light is."

Josiah helped. Unwillingly, from the scowl on his face. Then sat down.

"Perhaps you like to be clear of the ladies and assist Trac outdoors with the chores." She said pointedly.

To his credit Josiah raised himself up from the chair he was occupying and straightened his coat. "Of course." He said politely, but his face told a different story. After a few whispered words to Janie he made himself scarce.

"Good. Now there, Janie come and sit. We have materials to make gifts."

Before the hour was up, there was a huge pot of beef stew simmering and two loaves of bread rising.

Louisa reached down into another old flour bag and pulled out a stack of cut-out gowns. "For the little one." She smiled and then pulled out two pairs of tiny knitted baby booties. "These as well."

Janie stood, eyes filled with tears and Louisa could not help herself. She reached out and took Janie's frail body into her arms noting her thin shoulders. That act filled her with purpose. "While you gals are setting things up, I'm going to bake us an apple cake." Louisa announced as though it had been part of the plan. If you've got flour and grease I brought dried apples. Janie you must have something more than just stew." She said hoping the smell of cinnamon and apples might appeal to her hunger instincts.

By the time the cake was well nigh unto being done, Virginia had the makings of a tiny doll made of cloth and yarn for the new baby to play with. "I'll draw the eyes and the mouth with my charcoal pencil."

Once Louisa joined in things moved along until there was a small stack of gowns for the newborn. Janie had taken a needle in hand and began making tiny stitches as she hemmed each one.

"I haven't sewn in such a long while. I always hated sewing but now..." her voice trailed off and she smiled contentedly.

"The cake is nearly done. I'll mix brown sugar and butter with flour mixed in for a topping."

"It smells good."

Louisa smiled. Janie actually looked hungry and the light in her eyes began to appear.

The ladies stopped for a taste of the stew and some bread and butter, saving the most for supper when the men came in later. Daylight was burning away. Grace having been fed twice, now lay mewling on her palette near the fire. She was happy to flip over now and again as she played with a cloth toy, seeming to enjoy being in the middle of the commotion.

As darkness approached, they hardly noticed until Trac and Josiah came stomping up the steps beating the snow off their boots. A whoosh of wind followed them in, sending little scraps of yarn in every direction. The girls scattered to pick up their wayward items and with their looks told the men they were quite unsatisfied with their presence. Trac shrugged and looked at Josiah.

"Sorry, ladies. Sure smells good in here." Trac clapped his hands together after tossing his work gloves on a side table.

"Supper's done but we have to finish up and clean the table off." Louisa said pointedly. "I'll dish up Janie's men a plate first and you can take it down."

"Yes ma'am" this from Trac.

Glad for the aversion, he went back down to the barn with plates full of steaming food then returned to the warmth of the house.

Trac noticed Janie's face when she looked up. Tired but contented. It did his heart good to know she was up and doing something. He had worked Josiah harder than the man wanted to work, but seeing Trac wasn't going to quit, the four men pulled together, repaired a hole in the barn where one of the cattle kicked it through, cleaned up stalls and refreshed water and feed. And they scored a wide path through the snow from the barn to the house.

With barely any available space the two men leaned against the outside wall for a few minutes until finally they turned over a couple of water buckets and sat on them.

Reluctantly, for no woman could keep a hard-working man from eating, Louisa pushed herself away from the table and stretched, "I'll get supper dished up."

Instantly both men were on their feet.

Janie, slowly pulled herself up from the table. I'll help."

"I'll get the bowls and you can spoon up the stew." Louisa's voice was sweet.

Trac stood to the side and wished to be outside again. Except that darn food smelled so good, he could hardly keep his mouth from watering. He was glad when Louisa asked him to reach out and get the milk from the porch. "It should be cooled by now. We set it out a bit ago."

Trac and Josiah stayed out of the way knowing that getting in the way of a woman when she was cooking was nigh the same as taking eggs from underneath a sitting hen. Soon everyone found a place at the long narrow table.

"Don't forget to pray." Virginia said shyly.

"Of course dear." Louisa looked to Trac.

Everyone bowed their heads except Josiah, who sat like a stone grave marker.

"Lord thank you for this bounty, for friends, for family, for this home. Bless this house and all that's in it." He finished.

Within a moment chaos broke out as everyone started talking at once, helping themselves to the vittles.

Once everyone had eaten their fill, including apple cake, Virginia joined her sister on a corner of her palette and closed her eyes while Louisa cleared the dishes away.

Trac felt stifled in the small cabin. Janie looked helpless and he wanted to comfort her. Josiah left no room to do that because he was suddenly attentive to her every movement. Trac pulled on his duster and went outdoors where he could breathe. It was early evening but winter-dark.

He jerked in an icy breath and released it, and looked up. There, high in the midnight blue sky was a full moon shining in illustrious reflection upon the snow. He knew from Josiah's conversations this afternoon that he and Janie were as good as married as soon as the child arrived. Try as he might Trac's heart could not warm to the idea. He wondered if Janie had any feelings for the man. How could she? After Billy. He doubted it sincerely. But a woman without a man was trouble, especially in the wild Montana Territory. The only solution was for her to marry.

Louisa shooed Janie off to rest while she washed the dishes. Josiah, his hands spread across his midsection, groaned and took a seat. Once the house was in order, Louisa called to her brother who had just come in bringing the fresh smell of frozen air with him. The fire fluttered as the wind came swirling through the open door.

"Trac, I'm about done in and the girls are asleep. Would you mind if we spent the night? We could bunk down near the hearth . . . if you don't mind." She added.

"Are you sure there's enough room in here Louisa? I mean after all..."

"Josiah is going home." She stated firmly.

"I've had enough excitement for one day and I'm tired." He yawned, running his fingers through thinning hair.

"All right then. Horses are in the barn along with the sleigh. It'll save a trip back tonight, but we'll have to leave early so I can get back to the ranch."

Josiah put on his duster and with barely a word, slipped out the door, picked up his mount and headed down to the main road.

Trac watched the lone hunched figure descend down the lane, the horse plodding slowly through the falling snow, then turned from the window. He had asked Trac to watch out for Janie for the next few days because he had an obligation in Helena that he must attend to and would be gone for ten days, maybe more, which meant he would probably miss the birth.

"I suspect he doesn't want to be here when Janie's time comes." He murmured.

"Indeed." Louisa's curt answer told him she'd heard. "All the better..."

He had agreed and was now obliged. He would have to arrange something, since Janie refused to stay with her mother.

After an hour checking on things in the barn, he swept the porch clean of the new snow and let himself in trying not to let the door open too wide lest he wake everyone with the icy blast, which was picking up to high speeds now.

Louisa was tiptoeing around. "You can sleep near the fire. I've moved the girls in here so they'll stay warm. I'll sleep in with Janie, but leave the door open so I can hear the children."

He accepted two blankets and folded one to pillow his head, checked on the girls, and took his place on the wood floor. Louisa blew out the gas light and he was asleep in minutes.

The wind whistled without but within everyone was warm and safe.

Trac was up before light. He and his sister had already had their first cup of coffee when the girls began to stir. An hour later, sunshine bright in their faces as it reflected on the snow, there were several trips to the outhouse. Trac had already swept the new snow from the path so they could make their way to the necessary.

"Riley and Cash are here to shore up the lean-to outback. It about to tumble." He told Louisa. "We'll be working on that most of the day. They brought word that the men will take care of the stock today, so when you ladies are ready to get home, whistle."

Virginia clapped her hands. "We can stay longer, mama?"

"Yes dear we can, so let's make the most of it. We'll set up and get as much done as we can. And there will be no need to cook, we have plenty from yesterday."

Janie appeared in her bedroom doorway with a tired smile on her face.

"You look good, I must say." Louisa commented.

"I feel better today. Do you think we can finish our projects?"

"If we stay organized. I'll work on the quilt...Virginia can help. She is very good with her stitches."

Janie gasped when she saw the beautiful patchwork quilt Louisa pulled from her bag.

"It's beautiful." Her hands were traveling over the material.

"It's for you Janie." Louisa's voice trembled against her will.

Janie left the room and Louisa guessed she knew why. Janie had not wanted the baby from the first, even though it was a part of Billy. She had no desire to live anymore, let alone care for a child.

Before long Janie was back and Louisa carried on as though she'd never left. "Now which of you want to help?"

"I will." Janie replied unexpectedly. Virginia was playing with her sister.

Louisa scooted her chair close so they could each work a corner.

Hours passed and the lively chatter and busy hands made light work. There was much conversation about what Janie should name her child. It was finally decided: if a girl, her name would be Willa after her father William. If a boy, nothing less than William would do. But they would not call him Billy. He would be called Will.

Louisa hated that the day should have to end, but end it would. "Girls, Janie's about had her fill of a full household. It's time for us to go home."

Louisa wondered if it were true, such a look of loneliness passed over Janie's face.

She leaned in and whispered to Janie, "Would you rather come with us?"

"No. No. Josiah will be here today before he goes to Helena and he will want to be alone." She sighed. "He's not much for company."

"Josiah could stop at our cabin to visit you. It's closer than here..." Louisa offered.

"No, but thank you." Janie sighed.

"All right then." Spoken cheerfully.

As though on cue, Trac, Riley and Cash came bursting through the door, rubbing their hands together. "Man it's cold out there, even with the sun shining. We could use a cup of hot coffee and a bit of that apple cake, if there's any left." Trac stomped his feet.

Louisa and Janie set about pouring steaming streams of coffee in three tin cups and added a bit of cake to each plate, which disappeared as soon as it was served.

The wonderful visit had come to an end.

Trac stepped outside and came back in carrying a large item wrapped in a blanket. He set it down in the corner. "For the baby."

No one moved for an instant and then Louisa said, "Why is that a..." She pressed her fingers over her lips.

Janie moved slowly and bent over, removing the cover.

"The women gasped." It's a cradle." they all said at once.

Louisa, Virginia and Janie stepped closer to inspect it. "It's beautiful." This from Janie.

"Now you'll have a place to store your garments and use those blankets we sewed up." Louisa said watching Janie's eyes.

Janie set her heavy body onto a chair, her eyes bright. She turned and said, "Thank you Trac.

He noted, that for the first time in months, she looked him in the eye and said his name. His heart just about jumped out of his chest. He'd wanted that, yet wished she hadn't done it.

"Well, we'll be going now." Trac knew his voice sounded gruff and hollow in the silence, as he shifted from one foot to the other. "Will you be all right?"

Louisa broke the dreadful silence, "Josiah will be here today then?"

Janie nodded. "Yes." Tears filled her eyes and Trac looked down at his feet as Louisa went to Janie and hugged her fragile body. Trac's guts tore at him. He wanted to do the same.

"I'll get the wagon." He ground out and was out the door, followed by Cash and Riley.

Within minutes the goodbyes and hugs had been exchanged, Louisa handed Virginia to Trac and picked up Grace. With one last worried glance, Louisa waved at Janie standing so pregnant and so alone in her doorway.

"Oh Trac, we shouldn't leave her here. Her time is so close."

"She won't leave. You know that. Besides Josiah's coming." He slapped the reins and followed Cash and Riley through the late sunlit afternoon, so beautiful, but he didn't even notice.

Chapter 25

Two days later an excited Josiah was beating on Louisa's door. It was midafternoon and the children were napping.

"What is it? She pulled open the door irritated at his banging and shouting.

"I think Janie's time is upon her and I'm going to Helena." He said nervously.

"What? How bad is it?"

"How should I know. I've never . . . well, I've never had to do this before." He stood embarrassed to the roots of his brown hair. After a pause, "Will you see to her, then?"

Louisa stared at him for a moment, and God forgive her he reminded her of a slithering snake. "You may be sure of it." She said firmly.

"Thank you most kindly. I'm off to Helena, then." His face a mask of professionalism again.

And right you are to be clearing out of here you old fraidy-cat. Louisa thought. Whatever Janie saw in Josiah Wilson she could not fathom. She could not see one redeeming quality about this man.

But there was no time for criticizing, she reminded herself and pulled on her coat. Dinner was already simmering in the pot over the fire. She hoped Trac was in his office. With a check of the sleeping girls, she made her way to the bunk house then her brother's office.

"Trac, Janie's time has come." She said without preamble.

Trac looked up and knew that firstborns, human and animal, usually took awhile. "I'll take you over." He said easily. "Josiah going to be there?"

"He's on his way to Helena."

"He's not staying around?" He knew the answer by the look on his sister's face.

With Wes' help the horses were saddled and the sleigh packed and ready to go. Virginia would stay with Wes and they would make pies. Trac handed Grace up to Louisa and winked.

"Trac Gage Cordera, this is no time to dawdle. Babies come quick sometimes, and she's over there alone." She scolded.

"Yes, ma'am." He slapped the reins and turned the conveyance toward the lane, glad that the snow had melted down and then frozen.

They rode along, the bells echoing gaily as though there were a great celebration. His usually unflappable sister was staring out ahead of them as though doing so would get her there sooner. Little Grace's face peeped out from her heavy wrappings. He smiled as she blinked against the sun.

"Are you afraid?"

"Yes, I am Trac. What if something goes wrong? This is Billy's child and...and..."

He paused, "There will never be another child of Billy's born into this world. I've thought about that a million times."

"Oh Trac. How you've suffered. I've been so worried about myself without Emmett here. And Janie treating you so shabbily. How have you managed?"

He said nothing.

"You love her don't you?" Louisa stated firmly, her nerves calming.

Trac dropped one of the reins and reached down to pick it up. "What do you mean by that?"

"Just what I said. Somehow in my heart I knew it all along, but when you gave her the cradle, I was sure of it."

His secret was exposed. His mind worked awhile before he said, "Do you think she knows?" A quick glance at his sister.

"How could she? Being so full of grief and bitterness...."

The air became still and all that was heard was the scratching of the sleigh's metal rails across the icy snow and the breathing of the travelers as puffs of air were sucked away by the gentle winds. The dark cabin came into view nestled against the snowdrifts, a small ribbon of smoke drifting from the chimney.

"Oh do hurry. I won't feel right until I know how far along she is."

Trac pulled up close and jumped down, took Grace in one arm and helped Louisa down with his other hand. "You go on in."

"Hey gal, you and I are going to get some fresh air." He walked Grace around in big circles stomping down the snow near the front steps and then walked a path to the outhouse.

When Grace's face became red, he carried her inside and took off her wrappings and hung them on a nail. Louisa had already laid out Grace's pallet. He set her down and heard the women talking in the bedroom, but there were no strange noises, he noted thankfully.

After what seemed an hour, Louisa appeared.

Her brother looked so bereft, she went to him immediately. "Everything is moving along. She's quite advanced. She and Josiah had words. Seems Janie decided at the last she wanted him to go get her mother, but he refused because he'd miss his coach to Helena. He came for us instead."

"Blast him." Trac paced the room. "Blast him."

"I'm just glad it worked that we can be here. Janie's mother is far too high-strung to handle the birth of her daughter's child. It would be a disaster, Trac. So we should be thankful for Josiah's faults; at least this once."

Trac just stared at her.

Louisa noted his eyes were black with anger. And after she realized the way her brother felt about Janie, she didn't blame him one bit. Best to stay busy. "Tear up these petticoats into strips, make sure to wash your hands with lye first. I'll need two pots of boiling water and you can roar up the fire, Janie is shivering, half in fright, half due to the door being closed."

"Well, then open it up."

"It will compromise her...her modesty." She said over her shoulder, wondering why he didn't already know that.

"Modesty is hardly appropriate at a time like this." He sputtered. "When a birth is about to occur, man or beast, things need to be in plain view so the helper can help."

"Now then aren't we the expert in birthing?" She teased, her face turning a slight shade of pink. "You may just have to take a dose of your own advice, if I need you to help me."

At that, Trac backed off and bent down to look out the window pane; anything to avoid the look in Louisa's eyes.

"Just as I thought." She disappeared into the bedroom again.

Trac set to work tearing the strips and hauling the water in for the pots. The bedroom door stood ajar and he could hear them talking quietly. Nary a word came from Janie's mouth until about noon. Then things began to happen. At first there were quiet groans and then an hour later they grew louder.

Louisa had come out twice to feed Grace, barely noticing him. He was more than happy to entertain Grace. When she fell asleep he reached for his coat to head out to the barn. He heard horses.

Who could that be? He stared through the window. In a minute he was talking with Cash and Tan. They had come for Louisa.

"What's wrong out here?" Louisa stuck her head around the doorway, hearing the commotion.

Trac went to her. "Louisa there's been an accident . . ."

"Accident? Emmett?" Her eyes darkened.

"No, it's Virginia. She has fallen into the fireplace and burned her hand and broken her arm."

"Oh no. Louisa's hand went to her mouth. I must go to her." She turned and Trac grabbed her shoulders and turned her to face him.

"I'll go to Virginia. You stay with Janie." He ordered and leaned in to make sure they were eye to eye. He let her go and grabbed his coat.

"She's my child and I will go to her." Louisa stated firmly, her voice shaky. "I will tend to her. You will have to stay with Janie, Trac. That's the way of it."

"No, you stay, I'm sure Virginia will let me tend to her." His voice level heightened.

Louisa's eyes filled with tears. "Get the sleigh ready. I'll wrap Grace."

Trac knew there was no use arguing.

"Boss we can drive her back in the wagon and leave one of our horses for you. It'd be faster than putting her on horseback."

"Do what you have to do." Trac ran his fingers through his hair.

He knew by the looks on his men's faces that it was bad. Louisa must have known, too.

He watched them pull away and heard Janie moan loudly.

"God help me. Please help me." He groaned aloud and remembering what Louisa said, went to the washbowl, rolled back his sleeves and cleaned up to his elbows with lye. He tied one of Janie's aprons over his trousers.

Slowly, he pushed the door open and immediately his eyes fell upon Janie thrashing upon the bed, her hands tight around the bars at the headboard.

He pulled in a deep, shaky breath and walked slowly toward her. What in the world was he supposed to do now? Louisa had told him two things to do as she put her coat on, but he couldn't remember.

Janie moaned again and he stepped closer. Her nightgown was damp and her dark hair lay in a disheveled heap under her head.

"Louisa, Louisa." She called out. "I'm so cold." Her eyes were squeezed shut in pain.

He grabbed a blanket and spread it over her body, her stomach stretched out big. He lay his hand over it the way he did when cattle birthed and felt the baby writhing inside. "Thank God." He heard himself say. "Janie, honey, what can I do for you?"

For a moment she didn't speak, but bore another hard pain. When it passed, she ground out, "My hair, it's stuck." She said between breaths.

He reached back and lifted her head. A thick hank of hair was tangled around the post. He untangled it and swept up a handful and tied it with a strip of petticoat he'd torn.

"Better?"

"Oh yes." She mouthed before another pain tore through her. He doubted, in her advanced stage that she hardly knew who was attending her.

Another pain came quickly and overtook her. She kicked the blanket off. He reached for it and lay it over her again.

"I can't do this." She opened her eyes wide in a panic. "I can't do...." Another pain.

"Janie, look at me." Trac leaned down, hands on either side of her face, and said it again only with more force. "Janie, look at me."

She did. Her eyes were wild with pain.

"You are going to do this. You and I are going to do this, you hear?"

She wrangled and twisted like one of his calves when they were branding it. He waited for the pain to subside.

"Tell me what to do?" She begged "I can't do this."

"Yes you can. The only way to get this child born is to push it out. Now keep looking at me. When a pain is about to overtake you, look straight at me." He ordered.

"Okay, okay." Her eyes locked with his.

He tore her hands away from the bed posts and held them in his strong ones. "Now squeeze as hard as you can when the pain comes."

"Okay, okay, here it comes." She panted.

"Look at me, Janie. Squeeze. Harder."

Her frantic brown eyes flew to his and held. She blinked and shut her eyes against the pain.

"Open your eyes, Janie."

She did. "Now there's a good girl. Is it passing now?"

"Yes." She mouthed.

Another pain overtook her so suddenly and so soon it frightened Trac half to death. This time she yelled, "I have to scream."

"Then scream." He yelled back.

A loud, long wail came from deep in her gut and seemed to last forever. "The baby's coming." She said.

He knew what to do. Instinct kicked in. Reaching down he pushed the blanket back. There was a dark head.

"I can see it, Janie. The hair is black. Just like Billy's." He said excitedly.

"You can see it?" She was wet with perspiration and having lost his hands, had once again grabbed the bars above her head.

Suddenly her head went back and she yelled again. This time the tiny body slid out of her womb and into his hands. "It's here." He said staring at the tiny little baby laying across his arm.

"It's here?" She laid back in exhaustion. "It's here?"

"Yes, it's a girl, Janie. A girl." His voice was ethereal. He knew he was doing this wonderful thing, but felt like he was in another world.

"A girl? Lift her up, Trac. Let me see her."

He did, careful not to entangle the cord. He laid the squiggling baby girl across her chest and rubbed the top of Janie's belly as he did his cattle.

Both of them stared at the miniature human. Janie's hands roamed over the tiny arms and legs. She smoothed the baby's dark hair. Trac was touching the baby, too, making sure she was all right. Their fingers met at the top of the baby's head and Trac looked into Janie's beautiful brown eyes. She looked away.

"I'll tie the cord off ." He moved to get the clean strips, tied off the cord in two places and slit it in two with his pocket knife. Immediately he went back to business. In a few minutes the afterbirth was delivered and Janie took a deep breath and wept.

Hating to see her cry, but knowing females went through these sort of things, he kept working. "I'll wrap her up to keep her warm and we'll get her washed up."

"I'll wash her Trac. You've done enough." She started to lift herself.

"You'll do no such thing." He pushed her shoulder. "You need to be taken care of this time. Stay abed, this is one thing you can't do on your own Janie."

He heard the gruffness in his voice and saw the light go out of her eyes.

She lay back and turned her face away. Why had he been so harsh. She'd just had a baby, Billy's baby. Wasn't that enough for her to deal with? He admonished himself as he forced himself to keep working.

"Where are your gowns? Well get you and the bedding changed and then you can nurse." He said as though he did this every day of his life. She pointed.

Janie's face turned red. In spite of what they'd just been through, she was totally embarrassed. But there was nothing to be done. She allowed him to lift her from the bed and change the sheeting. He turned his back while she slipped off her gown and put on a fresh one.

In a few minutes the deed was done and she was back in bed. He rushed about the room cleaning up and bringing water to wash the baby. For now she lay wrapped in her mother's arms.

"Bring the cradle." She said softly.

He brought it in and placed it near the bed for later and lay the baby at the foot of the bed carefully. With dabs of warmed water he washed the tiny body from head to foot, gently squeezing water on her and then wiping it away.

Janie watched in awe at his gentle ways and careful handling of the baby. Even with his big work-worn hands. Her heart and conscience burned within her breast. She had so hated this man.

He wrapped a length of soft material around the child's bottom and tied a knot at the front.

"Like this?" he looked up.

"It'll do." She smiled softly

She waited as he went to bring a square of soft cloth that Louisa and the girls had sewn and wrapped the baby tightly inside and handed her to her mother. "You feed her. I've done all I can." He sighed loudly and sat down hard in a chair.

Janie looked down at her child. She was so beautiful. Dark like Billy, Her tiny mouth so like his. Tears sprang to her eyes.

"Something wrong?" Trac jumped up.

"No, it's just that . . . she's so beautiful."

He leaned down. "She is at that." He agreed, taking a tiny flailing fist in his hand.

129

Janie looked up for a moment and Trac's eyes met hers with a tender look. Quickly she looked down. It hurt her terribly to experience the guilt she felt in her heart. Not only for the way she treated Trac but for the fact that she had wanted to die, never caring for the life she carried inside her.

Trac backed off and busied himself in the other room while she fed the baby.

Janie and her baby did not know each other well yet, and at first she was not sure exactly what to do, but soon the baby showed her what she wanted and went after her mother.

Once they'd gotten the hang of it, Janie watched in awe as her daughter took nourishment from her body. She cuddled the tiny head next to her breast as tears of relief fell in rivulets down her face.

Chapter 26

Night fell around the cabin on the snowless night. Janie had fallen asleep with the baby in her arms. Trac took the sleeping bundle and put her in the cradle so Janie could rest. Oddly the cabin was quiet. He stoked the fire and sat in the rocker, put his head back and with eyes closed to the world relived the afternoon's activities. Strange, how one day could change a person's entire life. First, the day Billy died. And now this.

He prayed for Virginia, knowing that if they had not come for him, all must be well.

"Lord, thank you for today. You've brought about such a miracle and allowed me to be a part of it. Take care of Janie and her child, and Virginia too." He whispered before falling asleep.

Some time later, his body jerked to wakefulness . . . he heard a mewling. A cow in the barn about to give birth? What? Coming to himself he realized it was Janie's baby. He rose quickly stumbling as he went. Janie was up standing over the cradle about to retrieve her infant when she swooned. He could not get to her quickly enough but thankfully she just melted to the floor in a heap, her head missing the wood bedpost by inches.

He rushed to lift her. With the baby out of her body, she felt too light. Placing her gently on the bed he felt his heart speed up. Had she pined herself to death in grief? Just because she'd grown large with child they had assumed she was well. Looking closer, he pushed the sleeves away from her wrists and exposed her arms. They were thin. Too thin. So were her legs. She was wasting away.

A damp cloth to her head brought her back around. "What happened? She whispered hoarsely.

"You swooned."

"What?"

"You dropped from exhaustion. You're too weak and with feeding the baby, you'll need to stay abed and rest. And eat."

"But I need to care for her."

"I'll do it. You just tell me what you want. If you don't get stronger she won't make it, Janie."

Janie's eyes told him he'd been too frank. "Sorry, it's just that you never listen to anybody."

She turned her face away, wanting to cry and not knowing why. "Just leave me alone."

He did.

He made tea and toasted some bread over the fire, added lots of jam and brought it to her after a time. He knew not to bear down on her. New mamas seemed to be more fussy after calving. This was probably no different.

"Tea." He handed her the cup. Her hands shook but she put the cup to her lips and sipped.

"Thank you."

"Toasted bread and jam?"

"That does sound good."

"Eat up and I'll make you more if you want."

She ate in silence her eyes traveling between her sleeping newborn and Trac standing over the cradle peering down from his tall frame.

"She doesn't cry much." He whispered.

"Trac, what happened to Louisa? I know something's wrong because she never would have left me."

"Virginia fell into the fireplace, burned herself and broke an arm."

"Oh no." Tears sprang to her eyes. She knew a moment of motherhood at that instant. Your child being hurt.

"I haven't heard anything and it's been hours . . . one of my men would have come for me and brought your mother here if Louisa needed me."

"I tried to get Josiah, but . . ."

"Yeah, I know. He had his journey to worry about." Trac grumped.

Janie looked ashamed.

"Don't worry about it. Everything turned out all right. He'll be back in a few days and then you two can get married."

Janie looked up. "Married?"

"That's what he said." Trac was not kind.

"I see."

"It will be good for the child. She'll need a father."

"Yes." Came the whisper from the bed.

* * *

Trac slept on the floor near the hearth so he could stretch out and wished like crazy he could put himself to work outdoors. Most of the night he lay awake with his hands intertwined behind his head, half waiting to hear the baby, half thinking about the wonder of seeing a child born. Billy's child, the few moments of joy he and Janie shared together. Being a realistic man, he knew it was over. Janie would marry Josiah and that would be the end of it.

He could see now that little girl deserved a father and a mother . . . who loved her and each other. Janie could never love him like that. And the child would never know the bliss of happy parents. He could wait for Emmett to come home and go back to Texas. It was cowardly, but he doubted he could abide seeing Janie marry Josiah and live on Billy's ranch.

Before dawn he gave up trying to sleep. Besides he could hear the little one making noises. She would wake her mother and as long as she wasn't howling from hunger, he'd best go in and get her. Walking lightly across the wooden floor, he brought the candle closer and set it in the window sill in Janie's room.

The baby was wide-eyed, kicking her miniature feet. The cradle rocked slightly. She had kicked loose of her coverings and was having the time of her life. For awhile he watched. Only hours ago she'd been safe and warm inside her mother and now she was in the world heedless of harm or danger.

He wrapped the blanket around her wiggling form and gathered her up in his arms carefully. She was so tiny. In the crook of his arm, he carried her out in the other room. Janie had not moved.

Taking a seat in the rocker he soon realized she needed a fresh diaper. After the change he threw the old one in a half-full bucket of water, not knowing what else to do with it and returned to his seat. She lay on his knees and he watched her. Her eyes were open and she seemed content enough to lay and look about.

"Hey little one, you don't even have a name yet. What will your mother call you? Charity or Faith or what? You are a miracle. His quiet voice was almost a prayer. "God bless this child and whoever will raise her." He stumbled over the words, knowing his heart was not in touch with his prayer. His throat became tight and tears formed; the first time he could remember in a very long time.

What was this about? She was just a baby and he had two nieces, not to mention a little sister. But this child was different. She was Billy's own flesh and blood. Billy was no longer in the world and yet a part of him lay in his lap. Shaking his head he sat in awe, his eyes never leaving her.

Noting movement he looked up. Janie stood unsteadily hanging onto the door frame. Quickly he deposited the child on his pallet and went to Janie.

"She's fine, go back to bed." He chided, half expecting her to fuss. "She'll call out when she's ready for you. I told you to call me when you wanted to get up."

"I did, but you didn't hear."

"Oh sorry." He stuffed his hands in his pockets.

"I guess I'm kind of hoarse from all that screaming."

"I'd scream too, if I had to do what you did."

She barely reached his shoulders standing in bare feet. With a suddenness that made her dizzy, he reached down and swept her up into his arms. She let herself relax and laid her head on his shoulder. The beating of his heart beneath her ear sent her already sensitive emotions into a tailspin.

He lay her ever so gently back in bed. "Use the chamber pot and I'll come back in with the baby. Can you manage?"

"Yes." She said face flaming.

He helped her to a sitting position and then left her to tend to business.

In a few minutes she called. "Trac I'm ready."

He lifted the featherweight child and brought her to her mother, then turned to leave.

"Would you mind making another cup of tea? It sounds so good."

Glad to make an exit he made for the door with a nod and took an extra-long time to make it, giving her some privacy.

When he came to the door she was just readjusting the child to the other side. "You can leave the tea on the table."

He came in placed the tea on the table and retreated quickly. He heard the sleigh.

With a whoosh of wind and blowing snow, Louisa came through the door. "Oh Trac how did it go? Is Janie all right? What about the baby, was there trouble?" she asked all at once.

"Everything is fine." Give me your coat and go see for yourself."

He sounded so calm, Louisa stopped mid-question and stared at him. You sure everything is all right?"

"Everything's fine. How is Virginia?"

"Her arm is broken in one place and she burned the outside of her forearm, but she's resting. The doctor came in all this snow and set her bone, leaving a bit of laudanum which will keep her sleeping for some time, Doc said."

"Where's Grace?" He asked alarmed.

"Wes stayed with the girls. I fed her before I left and drove myself. I must get back, but I had to come."

Trac understood. Having a baby was no small thing out in this wild country; women had a special sense about the entire birthing process. He'd only just gotten a glimpse of what it was all about.

Trac took Louisa to Janie and watched as she kissed the baby's head.

He walked away and could hear all the 'oohing and 'aahing. They were so expressive. Men would hardly desire or dare to express themselves so openly.

He was beginning to feel like a father himself. He shook the cobwebs from his fuzzy brain, knowing that lack of sleep was the culprit. While Louisa was here he took the time to walk down to the barn and check the animals.

"I wondered where you were." Louisa's voice was sing-song happy as he walked through the door. "Janie told me all about it, Trac" She looked up at her brother. "I have to go. I'll be back tomorrow."

"Tomorrow? I've got to get going Louisa. Can't you work something out? I'll bring you and girls over and you can stay here for a few days."

Louisa knew now that her brother was overtired. "Trac, Virginia can't travel and I have to feed Grace."

"Oh, right."

"You're going to have to stay at least one more day. Could you call on Mrs. Preston? She could come."

"Right. Send Wes to bring Mrs. Preston."

"Wes is upset. Virginia was hurt while they were making those pies. He feels responsible. It'll be good for him to get away a few days while Virginia heals."

Trac breathed a sigh of relief.

"It may take a day or two to convince him." Louisa glanced at her brother. "He's set on taking care of Virginia."

"Well, tell him I can't stay here." Trac ran his fingers through his hair.

"I will do my best." Louisa smiled, knowing her brother was chomping at the bit to get out of there.

"Meanwhile, make sure she eats."

"She's been eating." He grumped. "Good thing you brought something. I was running out of ideas."

Louisa shrugged into her coat. "Don't forget to heat the soup until bubbling. And cornpone is wrapped in the towel."

He nodded.

She gazed into his bloodshot eyes and smiled. "Everything will work out."

"I know. It's just hard to stay in the house, when I know I have so much to do at the ranch."

"Your guys are picking up the slack. You need to let them sometimes, Trac."

He gazed at her not understanding in the least what she was talking about.

"Go eat something, feed the girls, and take a nap."

"Nap?"

You can take the time. You've no place to go." She goaded him.

"Just see that Wes gets here as soon as he can." He snatched the towel off of the table and burned his hand when he grabbed the blazing hot spoon from the soup pot. "Blast."

Louisa took her exit, a prayer on her lips and a smile on her face. "Thank you Lord."

Chapter 27

W es had taken his time getting to Janie's. Two whole days in fact. By the time Trac got out of Janie's house, he was so confused, he couldn't remember what day it was.

Three weeks passed while he wondered how Janie and the baby were doing. He threw himself into work like a man on fire, glad to fall into his bunk at night and fall instantly asleep. The last two nights he had stayed awake frustrated with himself for his inability to fix the problem that lay raging in the back of his mind.

One day he believed Janie would be better off with Josiah, the next he didn't know for sure. Praying constantly, yet remaining confused, he'd finally given up and left it with God. Whatever would be would be. At least that was his plan until he talked to his sister.

He was up at her cabin last evening when she caught him by the sleeve and whispered.

"Josiah's back."

"I know." He grumped, slamming his coffee cup on the table hard enough to slosh the hot liquid over the top.

"So why haven't you been to see Janie?"

Staring at Louisa . . . "Do you have to ask?"

"I'm asking aren't I?"

"What good would it do?"

"What good will it do to put it off?" Her hands were resting at her waist.

"It'll give her time. That's what. She needs a stable home, a man to watch over her, be a father to the baby."

"Her name is Willa."

"Who?"

"The baby."

"Willa?" he tried the name aloud.

"Janie named her Willa, like William. Willa Gage Cordera."

Trac stood, knocking his chair backward.

"That's right, Trac. She gave Willa your middle name to honor you for helping bring her into the world."

Trac paced.

"You didn't know?"

No answer.

"That goes to show where you've been."

He stopped pacing and stared at Louisa, his dark eyes black. "What's that supposed to mean?"

"Seems you've been avoiding the issue for weeks now. Doesn't give Janie much other choice but to marry Josiah Wilson, and he *is* making headway." She stared right back.

"Headway?"

"Yes. Heard he purchased a wedding band while he was Helena and brought some money back to build a cabin. A big one down by Tawny Lake."

Trac stopped pacing. "Why didn't I know about this? He demanded.

"You know now." She continued clicking her knitting needles, having decided to sit down so her brother could pace. He always did that when he needed to think.

Trac left the cabin in a hurry. Louisa got up and watched through the window as he stomped down to the bunkhouse. She smiled, sat down and picked up her knitting again. He didn't go for his horse; it was too late for that. But, she suspected, he'd taken to his bunk to mope around for awhile. But tomorrow, if he was half the man she knew he was, he'd ride over and tell Janie how much he loved her.

* * *

The plan was good but Providence does not always go along with the best-laid plans.

Sometime during the night Trac awoke, the smell of smoke assaulting his nostrils. He untwisted himself from the covers and opened the door. A sheet of flames hit him in the face. He slammed the door, broke out the window with his blanket-covered fist , climbed out and came in through the side door, yelling, "Fire! Get up! Fire!"

Suddenly there was chaos. The men began falling from their bunks half crazed from the smoke and wandering about aimlessly. It took them a few moments to realize what was what and they grabbed their blankets and ran out into the night in their long underwear. Someone thought to throw one on the snow so the men could stand on it in their bare feet.

Trac held the door open and shoved several men through and went back for Wes whose bunk was nearer the cooking area where the fire seemed to be strongest.

He yelled and yelled through the smoke and finally tore through the wall of flames, grabbing Wes by his clothes and jerking him out of his bunk.

"Wake up – get hold of yourself, we're getting out of here." He yelled through the popping sounds of fire eating wood.

Wes groaned but was able to walk with Trac shouting orders in his ear. Finally outside, Trac pulled in a deep breath and fell into a snow bank with Wes choking and coughing. They'd all made it out alive. Heaving great gulps of clean air into their raw lungs, they crawled away, watching from a distance as the bunkhouse burned to the ground.

Trac felt unusually calm under the circumstances. His men were accounted for and no one had been hurt. The flames hurled themselves viciously into the night sky. Then he heard a female voice behind him.

"Trac. Oh Trac." Louisa was running in her nightclothes, barefoot in the snow. He swept her up as she came crashing into him. "Thank God you're all right." She sobbed on his shoulder. "I thought you were still in there."

"Trac carried his sister back to the house. "Get back in bed and stay put." He ordered.

After he left she changed into a fresh gown and watched from the small panel window in her bedroom, tears running down her face.

After the shock that her brother was all right she began to sorrow at his material loss. "Trac, all your work..." Then caught herself. "Oh God, thank you for sparing these lives tonight. I don't know what I'd do if I lost Trac. With Emmett gone and Billy, too..."

Somehow the girls slept through all the chaos; but Louisa could not go back to bed. All she could see through the windows were the flames and Trac's bunkhouse burning. By morning the fire had eaten up the wood and there was nothing left but the stone fireplace, which was still standing against the dark blue sky as dawn crept up and revealed gray ash from the hearth blowing away in the winter wind.

Louisa, determined to busy herself, began cooking. The men would need breakfast – and clothing. Trac had taken the men to the cattle barn so they would be out of the wind. Louisa gathered all of Emmett's trousers and shirts and bundled them up, then dressed herself. Heavy snow was falling. Holding the rope that stretched from tree to tree led her from the house to the barn. No need to cause any trouble for Trac today by getting lost or frozen.

The barn door opened and several faces peered out from the darkness. The men had turned tree stumps into seats and sat huddled in their blankets in a stall that had been cleaned of straw. A small fire burned in a tin can...barely enough to warm the small space.

"Here I've brought clothes." She handed the bundle to one of the men.

"Come up to the house and get a meal. Give me a few minutes to lay out the table then you all come."

Trac came from somewhere in the back. "Thanks Louisa. We'll make out until we can get a wagon to Helena for supplies. John'll give us credit. We're making a list."

She nodded and hurried away. The children would be waking up and she would have to tell Virginia.

Half an hour later, Trac's men, all half-dressed, blankets covering their shoulders hurried in out of the elements. There was barely standing room. Louisa seated as many as she could fit, and handed the rest a plate.

No one said too much but ate heartily. Louisa cleared the plates and set to washing the dishes as Virginia carried plates with her one good hand.

"Men, we're all out safe, thank God for that; but we have to rebuild and in the dead of winter. Any ideas?" He looked around the table.

"I say we get four men in a wagon and into Helena today. It'll take a few extra days if they can't get through Stoney Pass, but the rest can stay behind and see about cleaning up so we can work on the foundation." Riley was speaking.

"Sounds like a fair plan. Who wants to make the trip?"

Cash, Dan, Tom and Riley decided to go while Tan, Wes and Trac would stay behind and start clean-up.

"We'll leave today." Riley took charge.

"You're sure?" Trac asked.

"Why not?" This from Riley.

"Long as you've got the strength. We'll lend you some of our shirts and trousers and coats and you can take extra blankets along. It's not going to be easy getting through the Pass, and if you can't the trip'll take two extra days. You'll need plenty of food in case another storm comes in."

Riley nodded. Trac was glad he was determined.

"Dan." Trac continued, "you and Tom can ride over to Mrs. Preston's, see if she kept any of her husband's clothes. I'll ride over and see if Wilson can give us a hand. Wes, you stay inside and rest. You got the worst of it. Maybe Louisa could use a hand at supper. The men will be needing something hearty."

"You bet, boss" Wes' deep voice was hoarse from the smoke.

The house began to clear.

"Louisa," Trac whispered, "Don't let Wes overdo. He doesn't look too good."

Louisa went about her work as though nothing had been said. She knew how to handle sensitive issues.

* * *

The men scattered, each knowing what their jobs were. Trac saddled Job. Tan ended up alone and went out to survey the damage and get as much cleaned up as he could. Trac loaned him his coat and wore the thinner one with a horse blanket thrown over his shoulders.

He saw Josiah Wilson's wagon at Janie's and it was not even mid-day. What was he doing here, unless...he'd been at Janie's all night.

He pulled in a breath and banged on the door. Hard.

When Janie opened he spit out, "Wilson here?"

"Yes, he just rode in." Janie replied as she opened the door further. Josiah Wilson sat at Janie's table eating biscuits and sipping coffee while reading the *Helena Independent*. He laid it down and with a smug look on his face said, "Janie, dear, pour me another cup." He held the cup up.

Without a word she reached for the pot. Trac watched her emotionless and fluid movement as she poured. She was dead inside. It had been months since Billy's death and still she had not returned to the woman he knew her to be. Trac wanted to cry.

Instead, he felt anger rise in his chest and slapped his borrowed frozen gloves against his thigh to remove the snow and spoke rudely, "I've had a fire at the bunkhouse, burned to the ground last night. We need some extra hands. Can you help us clean up?"

Trac heard Janie gasp.

"What? In this weather? Wait until spring, then I'll come." And with that he picked up his cup and slurped loudly.

The louse. Trac almost spoke the words aloud, but pressed his lips together when he saw Janie looking at him. Her dark eyes dropped to the floor.

So that's the way it was then? The spark had gone out of Janie Cordera. He had to get out of that stuffy house before he landed his gloved fist right into Josiah Wilson's pompous face. He turned to reach for his black Stetson and realized it was gone. Burnt in the fire. He pulled the blanket around his shoulders and opened the door.

"I'll come…to help Louisa." He heard Janie's small voice. He narrowed the opening to keep the snow out and turned.

"You'll do no such thing." Josiah stated emphatically.

Janie took a step toward Trac. "Did you bring the wagon?"

"No, just my horse."

"Oh."

"I can go back and get it Janie, just give me the word."

"Go and get it." She said and turned her back, leaving the men alone.

"I'll be back in a couple hours." Trac yelled over his shoulder and quit the house.

He could hear Josiah's tirade against Janie even before the door closed behind him.

Trac smacked his gloved hand on the porch post as he went by. "Lord, make her strong." He prayed and set his horse toward home. "By golly she still has a little spunk in her yet." He whooped out to the snow-covered hills.

Less than two hours later, he had the wagon back at Janie's, and was knocking at her door, fists tight at his side. Wilson answered the door like he knew he would and began his harangue all over again.

"You can't expect a new mother to take her newborn out in this." He waved his hand in the air.

"Janie's a grown woman. She can do as she pleases." Trac said evenly as Janie stepped out from her bedroom.

"I forbid it Janie. We have an arrangement." He hinted, looking the part of a politician speaking from the podium.

She ignored Josiah. Trac hid a smile behind his gloved hand.

Janie had the child wrapped until she looked more like a year-old babe than a newborn one, she was so thick. He peeked into the cradle and the tiny pink faced child was asleep.

"Do you have any of Billy's clothing? My men lost everything in the fire last night." He hoped the request would not set Janie off.

"Yes," She answered quietly and retrieved a huge bundle of Billy's shirts and trousers and handed them to him

"Any socks?"

"I believe so." She returned with a small bundle of socks which Trac took gratefully and thanked her with his eyes.

When all stood ready at the door, Trac went ahead and carried out the bundles then came back for Janie and Willa.

"You'll regret this Janie Cordera." Josiah said threateningly, his thumbs tucked into his vest pockets.

Janie looked him straight in the eye and Trac heard the grandest words ever. "Josiah, I've changed my mind about the arrangement. Please be gone when I return."

Trac made himself of no consequence by hurrying out the door. He took Willa, helped Janie climb into her seat, handed the babe up, then took his place.

"You warm enough?" he asked after a long silence.

"Yes, I am." She answered, her head down against the snow blowing in their faces.

No words passed between them for a long while as they rode over the packed snow. When the blizzard let up a bit she asked, "Are Louisa and the girls all right?"

"They're fine. Thank God it was the bunkhouse and not the barn with the wagons and cattle. Wes swallowed a gutful of smoke but he'll recover." Trac slapped the reins harder to hurry the horses.

When they arrived, Trac jumped down and helped Janie and Willa down then stood aside to let Janie pass.

"Oh my!" Louisa said, wiping windblown strands of hair away from her eyes. "Janie...I'm so glad to see you."

Trac had decided to surprise his sister in case Janie changed her mind.

"I've come to help."

"Here now, let me take Willa. I'll unwrap her and you can settle yourself." Louisa snuggled the baby close, kissing her feather down cheek. "I'll put her on Grace's pallet since Virginia is entertaining Grace on my bed."

Trac carried in the extra clothes and dropped them just inside the door. "Billy's clothes for the men." He said quietly and left the women to their own affairs. "I'll be down helping Tan."

Louisa waved him off and shut the door quickly. "At least the snow has stopped and the sun's come out." She hung Janie's coat on a peg.

The woman began their ritual of cleaning and preparing large loaves of bread and extra servings for dinner, chatting the hours away.

By the time evening came a hearty bean soup simmered in the huge wash pot – scrubbed clean for the occasion. Bread loaves were in the warming oven and dried apples with sugar and cinnamon bubbled over the fire, adding a welcoming fragrance to the cabin.

"When do you expect Molly back?" Janie asked.

"I'm just hoping Margaret doesn't keep her in Boston. Molly is so like Margaret, yet I wonder if she wants to come back to the land of the plains when there is so much to do out East."

"My mother came from Philadelphia."

"Why I never knew that Janie."

"She was quite the society woman."

"Oh tell me about it." Louisa continued working.

For an hour Janie talked about her mother's family. "She's so proper." Janie sighed. "I'm not at all like her."

"What on earth makes you say that?" Louisa laughed lightly. "You're very much a lady like your mother, just a bit more blustery."

"Blustery?" Janie laughed. "Maybe before, but not now." She grew serious.

Willa's cry called for her mother and Janie picked up her child and nursed her then rocked her back and forth, tipping her toes on the floor to add momentum. "She likes to be rocked hard."

"Like her father." Louisa smiled and scooted her chair close until she sat knee-to-knee with Janie.

"There's something I've been wanting to talk to you about... and since there are no men or little ears about . . .

Janie looked away and tears threatened. "I don't know why I cry so much, Louisa. Nothing's going to be different. Nothing."

"That's not true Janie." Louisa's sympathy only made Janie's tears run faster.

"You are beautiful, young, and strong...and Willa's mother. You have everything to live for. You have a part of Billy with you forever."

Janie contemplated her friend's words and nodded.

But Louisa saw her heart wasn't in it. "Janie, you've been so quiet these last few months...I miss you. The real you."

"Me, too Louisa. I have no life left in me." She hesitated . . . "not even with the baby." She sobbed at the awful confession.

"Oh dear Janie." Louisa slipped out of her chair and sat at Janie's knee. "Grief is so strange. It takes from you what you don't want to give.

"It has, Janie whispered, wiping her small hands across her face. "I just didn't know how bad it would be. I never thought Billy could die. He was so strong."

Louisa leaned her head down on Janie's knee. "I don't know what I'd do if I lost Emmett, Janie."

Just then a shaft of wind blew in, nearly sucking the air from the cabin as Tan and Trac entered. Louisa had not even heard them approaching.

"Oh," she exclaimed and jumped up to get supper.

The men pulled off their meager coats and set their boots by the fire to dry. "We're soaked to the skin." Tan said smiling. "But we got a lot done. Tomorrow we can get the foundation repaired."

"Good, now you two sit down and eat."

Janie excused herself to tend to the baby. Trac and Louisa exchanged glances.

Maybe Providence was working after all, Louisa thought.

Chapter 28

A week passed. Trac and Tan worked outdoors most days and enjoyed peaceful evening talks. Everyone in the house had ideas for the bunkhouse. The girls stating there should be installation of a bath house where the men could wash up and Wes needed a larger space to work in which should include a pump right outside the back door.

"That'll be nigh impossible until summer." Trac laughed. "At least the snow has shrunk down a bit."

"Trac why don't you and Janie take the rockers tonight." Louisa suggested that evening. "I'm tired and I want to turn in early. The men should be back in a day or two and we'll be needing to get food cooked up again. I need my rest." She yawned loudly. "Tan, you're welcome to sleep on the floor if you wish. Wes sure won't come up."

"No ma'am, thank you all the same. I'm cozy enough in the hay." He looked embarrassed, for ranch men were hardy souls. "Nosiree, think the barn'll suit me fine." He tipped his head politely before exiting.

Trac had slept in the barn with his men, but after a week working outside in the elements and sleeping in a freezing barn, it sounded mighty tempting.

Louisa's face colored. In her tiredness she was overcome with the lack of good sense. What was she thinking putting the two of them together? She headed for her bedroom where the girls were already asleep and climbed under the covers.

Janie checked Willa and took a seat in the rocker, picked up *Farmer's Almanac* from a stack of books.

"Lookin' to be a farmer instead of a rancher?" Trac smiled and grabbed a sheaf of paper.

"No. Just love to read."

"I didn't know. What other kind of books do you like to read?"

"Oh, I don't know. About faraway places, I guess." She sounded wistful.

"You mean like back East? Or like England, France, places like that?"

"Both."

"Well, I'll let you read then." He pulled out his knife and sharpened a pencil stub. "Gotta get another list together."

The sounds of her rocker creaking gently back and forth made Trac's heart beat faster. He wanted this woman and Willa making her baby noises sitting next to him in his own house for whatever time God gave them on this earth, which is exactly what he prayed for right there and then.

"Ask and it shall be given..." he said quietly.

"What?" Janie looked up.

"Just quotin' Scripture."

His heart had begun to hope about the time he saw Janie's head fall over. He caught the Almanac before it slipped out of her hands and laid it next to her on the floor, put a blanket over her, then made his palate by the fire and slept soundly.

* * *

He awoke to the sound of men's voices. Riley and his crew were back. Cash tapped at the door lightly while Tom, Dan and Riley took the wagon on down to the barn to unload. Trac threw on the only coat he had and pulled a blanket around his shoulders.

"Put breakfast on the table." He whispered to Louisa who had come half asleep from her quarters. "The men are back."

"Go on now." She waved him off. "I know what to do." And pushed him out the door.

Janie was already awake, had been snug in the rocker, her eyes closed as she heard the men and Trac talking quietly. Once Trac left she disengaged herself and fed a hungry Willa then helped Louisa set the table.

They'd made plenty of bread. Louisa fried a batch of bacon and eggs and set out butter and jam. Fifteen minutes later the house was filled to overflowing with hungry men.

Janie and Louisa served up food as fast as the men could eat. Louisa kept eggs cooking in the skillet. The men tried to be polite but it had been too many days since they'd had a real meal. They'd eaten only what they could catch on the trail, the money saved for supplies.

"Eat up gentlemen." Louisa encouraged and realized instantly they needed no provoking.

"Mighty thankful." Riley crowed between bites.

Trac watched as Janie passed a newly sliced loaf of bread and plates of eggs down the line. Her movements, so smooth and quiet, were unlike the old Janie. He knew her heart was broken and yet she was trying to help others. He knew it did her good. If only he could talk to her alone somehow. She was not as angry and hateful as she had been; but he didn't know how to make things better between them except to come right out and say what he was thinking. Janie would never understand how he had always loved her. He didn't trust himself and feared alienating her altogether so said nothing.

Chapter 29

The first logs were cut and laid on the foundation. The new bunkhouse was nearly twice the size of the old one. Several of the men suffered from frostbite, so Louisa insisted they work in shifts, coming in warming up then going back out. She wasn't going to take any chance that one of them might lose an appendage or get gangrene.

The new cook stove was installed and Wes began cooking breakfast under the lean-to the men built. The dismal winter days turned into weeks. Help came from neighbors just in time to lift the side walls. It had taken several days for the word to get around, but true to their nature, the neighboring men had come in a big wagon bringing their sons and tools along. After that it took no time until the roof was on and the bunkhouse was shelled up.

At the end of week two Louisa caught Trac after supper, "Janie wants to go home."

"All right. I'll take her tomorrow." He said tiredly and took off out the door. They were working by gaslight lanterns now, through the night, to get the work finished enough so they could build a fire and stay inside. They could build bunks and tables once the outside walls were up.

Trac was feeling the burden of trying to catch up in time for Spring roundup. The other men who'd wintered with their families would be back. All the ranch records and papers had burned in the fire. He knew he had to recount the stock, and that would take many man hours. He dreaded that job.

Early the next morning, Trac announced at breakfast he was going to take Janie home. He, Tan and Riley had worked through the night while Tom, Dan and Cash had slept in the barn. Today they would switch places. Tempers were growing thin.

"Wes would you mind making an extra plate for Janie? I don't want to wake Louisa to do it."

"Sure boss. Fact is, I've got plenty left over from breakfast this morning. I'll pack it up. 'Sides, she don't eat much."

"Thanks Wes. Appreciate that. I'll go up and get her and we'll stop by and pick up the food in a little while."

Trac trudged up to the house.

He knocked quietly. The house was unlit and quiet. Janie came to the door fully dressed.

"You ready?" he asked, eyes burning.

"Yes, I'll get Willa." She whispered without looking at him.

She hurried about and Trac settled his new Stetson on his head. It was still too stiff to suit him.

"Here have a cup of coffee." Janie pushed a cup into his gloved hand. She looked up at him for the slightest moment and he had the notion to take her into his arms and kiss her right then and there, but she had hurried away.

"Must be too tired." He mumbled.

"What?" Janie called softly from the dark corner. "You're always mumbling."

"Nothin'." He said and Janie could hear the tiredness in his voice.

"If you're too tired, Trac, one of your men can take me."

"I'll take you." He stated firmly.

She had a wrapped bundle to carry besides Willa. "Give her to me." He said gruffly and Janie obeyed. As she slipped the baby in his arms, Trac found himself pushing the blankets aside and peering into the face of a fully awake baby girl smiling at him.

He felt his mouth turn up at the corners, first time in days. "What're you doing up so early huh? Gonna be like your pa and be a little wild one?"

When he looked up Janie was staring at him.

"Something wrong?" he grumped.

152

"No." she said and turned her back, pretending to look for something.

Now what? He wondered. Had he said something?

The next thing he knew Janie had grabbed the bundle, opened the door and was headed out. He followed with Willa in one arm. He grabbed Janie's arm and helped her up then gave her the baby.

He bounced down hard on the seat. "Sorry."

They traveled in silence, then exasperated he tried again. "Did I say something wrong back there?"

"No."

"Then why does it seem to me I've upset you?"

"You did no such thing. It's just . . . just nothing."

"It ain't nothing or you wouldn't be sitting there with tears running down your face." He said firmly, tired of all the animosity between them.

"If I say it's nothing, it is." Janie said and he could hear the old bitterness creeping up again.

He slapped the reins and let it go, knowing he was too tired to argue and too weary to try and figure her out. By the time he got to Janie's he could feel a chill from her that hurt more than the icy snow biting into his face.

Her cabin was cold. He'd had to push the drifts away from the door to get in. Josiah Wilson could have cleaned up before he left. "You sure you are going to be all right? He asked for the second time.

"Yes, just need a fire going." Her teeth were chattering. She started toward the wood pile.

"I'll get it." Trac told her, irritation setting him on edge.

Janie shrugged and put on a pot to boil for tea.

Trac bent down on one knee and set the fire to raging.

"You don't have to burn us out of here." She said smartly.

Trac stared her down but said nothing as he stood to warm his hands. "Don't worry I'll be out of your way before you know it." The words sounded bitter even to his own ears.

Tears popped into Janie's eyes as she picked up the baby and soothed her crying, went to her room and slammed the door.

"You don't have to be so huffy." Trac yelled loud enough for her to hear. "I'm leaving. If you need anything," he paused, "I'll send one of the men to check on you."

"Don't bother." She yelled.

"Well, that didn't go too well, Lord." Trac said aloud, discouraged. A man can only take so much. The last few days had seemed to draw them closer and now this. "Fact is, I don't know what to do with that woman. I don't know how to stop loving her. You got any ideas, Lord?"

Whistling to keep awake, Trac forced himself to hum hymns. It always seemed to keep him from thinking too much. What he needed was sleep. He slapped the reins.

* * *

Louisa answered Trac's knock. She wasn't expecting anyone at mid-morning, especially since Wes was cooking for the men now.

"Could I use your bed?" he asked, eyes bloodshot and blinking to stay awake.

"Of course. I'll keep the girls quiet and you can get some rest. Heaven knows with all that pounding down there you haven't had any decent sleep have you?"

"Nope. And I'm tired of being cold." He stated as he pulled off his boots and pitched his coat and hat on the nearest hook.

She handed him an extra blanket, shooed the girls off the bed and heard the ropes squeak as her brother, all six foot two of him landed on her bed. He slept all day and though the night. Louisa and the girls camped out in the big room near the fire.

Next morning he appeared in the doorway, yawning and hair askew.

"Uncle Trac. You slept in the daytime and all night too." Virginia said surprised.

"I sure did honey." He scratched at his beard. When had he last shaved? He couldn't remember. "Wore out is what I was."

"Come and eat Trac." Louisa invited and he gladly found a chair.

After two cups of coffee and double helpings for breakfast, Louisa asked, "Janie make it home all right?"

"Yes, but not before we had words. I don't like her and Willa up there alone in the middle of winter."

Louisa's eyes softened. "Trac her two ranch hands are there. They can look in on her. You don't have to do it all."

"I know. I don't know what set her off, but I know we were angry with each other when we parted."

"Too much going on." Louisa muttered. "Things have settled down, now that the barn is shelled up and there's a warm place to work and food for the men."

"Yes, thankfully. But things are still unfinished between you two."

Trac stared at her. "What things? Janie will always think of me as the one who killed Billy. That's a fact, sis."

"Oh Trac, for pity's sake, have you no eyes?" She stood exasperated to the tips of her toes.

Trac could see she was about to go into one of her informational tirades that usually left him feeling guilty. Good thing he'd gotten some good sleep and coffee.

"Goodness knows you two are going to be the death of me yet."

Trac thought, but didn't say it, that his little sister was in the same condition he was in before he slept it off. "What does that mean?" he asked with caution.

"God can only work with willing souls." She sputtered. "And you two . . . well, it's nigh near hopeless."

"She spouted at me first thing." He defended himself. "What was I supposed to do? Act like a lilly-liver and sit there?"

"And so you did the same? Sassed her back? That was real mature, Trac."

He shrugged.

"I should've known. And I've made so much headway with her, explaining that you didn't mean for Billy to die...you only wanted him to win the nugget so he could build Janie her new home."

"You told her that?"

155

"Yes. It was the truth." Louisa's voice raised a level.

"Well, she sure didn't cut me any slack when I took her home."

"What do you expect her to do? She's dealing with the loss of her husband, Trac."

"She could start with being a little more cordial, tell me she's sorry for putting me through all this." He offered.

"You snake. You lowdown yellow-bellied snake." Louisa stood.

Now he was in trouble. Louisa never called him a snake. Especially not a yellow-bellied one.

"Well . . ." he started to speak but was interrupted.

"Well, nothing. How would you feel if say Wes did something, not on purpose, that ultimately caused me to die, like in that fire."

"Why I'd . . . "

"That's what I thought. Since when is Janie not allowed her grief and even her accusations if that's how she really feels?"

Trac rubbed his chin against his rough hand making a scratching sound. "For sure you got me there."

"Stop that!"

"Yes, ma'am."

"And stop that, too..."

"What?"

"Making fun of me." She declared pacing behind him.

Trac knew when he was beat. "All right. Fun over. What is it I did so wrong? Tell me straight out."

Louisa huffed. "Trac you and I both know you were not responsible for Billy's death, but Janie *thinks* you were and until you talk to her yourself and try to explain how things happened that day, she'll go on thinking it."

"You mean I should bring up the subject?" he was doubtful that would help. "She already knows what happened. I told her once and she screamed at me."

"That was the very first day she found out." Louisa shook her head. "She's had time to process. She's more open now. Grief does strange things to people, Trac."

"Didn't you already tell her like it was. It's better coming from you anyway."

"No Trac, it has to come from you. You have to make her understand, calm her fears, apologize for the part you did play in the bet and tell her gently, that Billy made up his own mind."

"You're asking a lot. I have no idea how to talk to a woman in grief."

"Especially one you love right?"

Trac looked up at her soft voice. "Right." He had to agree.

"Then you do love Janie?"

"Like my own life." He heard the weakness in his voice.

"Then let her know."

Trac shrugged again and Louisa cuffed him a good one across his muscular shoulder.

"Men."

He headed toward the door after stopping to romp a bit with the girls who were up. Virginia looked at him. "You know too don't you?" he said incredulously, when she asked if he were going to visit Janie soon.

"Women." He grumped, pulled on his boots, coat and hat and opened the door. Just in time to see Josiah Wilson's raised hand ready to knock.

"What did you say to Janie?" He demanded. "She's crying all over the house and nothing I say will stop her."

Trac shrugged. "None of your business, Wilson."

"I demand to know. She threw me out in a most unceremonious act."

"I think she told you to be gone the last time, if I remember correctly." He kept his voice low.

"I'm not an easy man to dump, Mr. Cordera." Josiah said proudly.

"I can see that."

"Janie and I had an agreement until you came that day and carried her off."

"What kind of agreement, Wilson?"

"An engagement, to be precise." He stated, pushing his chest out.

"Women break engagements."

"Not this one. I mean to build her a house and even take her child as my own." His puffery was obnoxious.

"Well, that is good of you." Trac growled.

"She will have a good life with me. I can offer her security, safety, and even raise that child."

"You've said that twice. He ground out. "Is there anything else before you go."

"With all due respect, I'm going to have to ask you to leave Janie alone."

"Can't do that." Trac's voice remained indifferent, surprising even himself.

"I think it is your best interest. I plan on asking her to be my wife...again – if she'll let me back into the house." He paused, "Women are such strange creatures . . ." his words fell away.

Silently Trac thought, *that is one point we can agree on.* "Give it your best shot." Trac said over his shoulder as he stepped past the man. "But don't expect me to cheer you on."

Trac stomped away, his heart beating furiously in his chest. So Wilson was going to ask her today. Should he get there and ask her first or let Providence move.

As life would have it, he could not get away. He pounded his hammer and sawed wood with a vengeance the entire day.

Thoughts chased through his mind like a hungry cat after the last mouse in the barn. What if she said yes to Wilson. She might, since she was so angry with him. He had been a bit touchy. Woe to him if he'd blown his chances with Janie for good. Perhaps she would find the good Mr. Wilson a better choice.

Well, it couldn't be helped. If she married him she did. He tried to reason it out but it was no good.

"Boss we got trouble here." Tan came riding up. "Seems we got a slew o' bogged cattle down by Curt's Hill.

"Get Dan and take care of it Tan." Trac yelled over his shoulder.

"Need more'n just two riders. It's pretty bad, seems a fence was trampled down and there's a lot of 'em."

"All right. You go on. I'll meet you out there."

Trac caught Riley and sent him to tell the bunkhouse crew while he grabbed his gear. "Well be splittin' off for awhile. Got trouble down at Curt's Hill. Have Wes rustle up some vittles."

"Need more help? Be quicker." Riley wanted to know.

"No, I need you here to keep things running smooth." Trac called out. Riley went back to work.

The three men headed for the hills glad the sun was shining and the snow melting. It was late afternoon before the bogged cattle could be found and nearing dark by the time they'd gotten them free. Each man was covered in mud by the time they returned to the bunkhouse.

"Seventeen of them. Ain't had that much trouble in a long time." Tan told the men later. "Boss sure was burnin' up about something though. Ain't never seem him so darn impatient. Why, he was lettin' go all afternoon. Not like him."

"Woman trouble, prob'ly." Wes said seriously. "Billy's woman. She's been causin' Trac trouble ever since Billy died. Blames him for it. And with everything going on here, he's been on the grumpy side. He cain't take care of Billy's ranch and this one, too and live to tell about it."

Trac walked through the door sputtering about something or other and the men quieted and kept working.

"No sense in making' any more trouble for him." Wes cut in.

Too tired to think, Trac dropped his muddy clothes in a pile, washed himself up and wondered if Janie had said yes or no to Josiah Wilson.

Chapter 30

With January and most of February gone, the bunkhouse was up and things were slowly coming along. Trac got a crew together and rode into Helena for more supplies.

"You know what you need to do." Trac told his men when they reached town. "We'll spend the night at Roscoe's Hotel and meet back here after breakfast. "I'm gonna check on hiring a couple of extra hands to get the bunkhouse finished and the countin' done.

They waved their hats and took off.

At the General Store, Mr. and Mrs. Kipper greeted Trac kindly. Their daughter, a dark-haired beauty, was smiling at him shyly from behind the counter.

"Ma'am," He tipped his hat to the women and greeted old man Kipper.

The smell of dill assaulted his nostrils. Mrs. Kipper stopped refilling the pickle barrel and made her way to the counter. "You know my daughter, Olivia, Mr. Cordera."

"Yes, ma'am."

Trac had eyes and could see Olivia Kipper was beautiful, but young.

"We've seen you at church several times, Mrs. Kipper continued. "The good Reverend Dunham was here only this morning and said what a beautiful daughter we have."

Trac's eyebrows raised at the bold insinuation but he ignored it. Perhaps it was high time he looked at another woman, come to think of it. Janie would never be his, especially the way things were going now. Perusing supplies, he took another look at the girl behind the counter. Her shiny black hair, braided and curled around her well-shaped head could turn a man's eye. And she didn't seem at all affected by her ma's pointed comments.

Olivia Kipper continued rearranging cans on the shelves. That suited him fine for now. He was in no mood to deal with another female. Quick as a rabbit he needed to get out of there. Tossing a few items on the wood counter, he waited until Mrs. Kipper wrote in her cash journal, then left quickly, the bells above the door ringing in his ears.

A visit to the barber and the home-cooked food at the hotel put him in better spirits. Several men in town sat down at the table and talked.

"Any ranch hands looking for work?" Trac asked loud enough for anyone to hear. If a man was looking for work, he'd speak up.

"Sure enough." One man replied. "there's a party of five here looking for work. We got sick of the gold diggin' and made up our minds to go home to our wives, all except for Joe here. He's not hitched. Snow shut the pass before we could get through."

"I can use three of you." He eyed the men as they made their way to his table. "Work is finishing off a bunkhouse inside and helping with the stock and chores on a neighboring ranch. Come Spring you'll be counting and branding cattle. Name's Cordera."

A groan came from a couple of the men, "Whoa, ranchin's not for me. Joe here, Hank, and Pete've done cattle ranching. Me and Sam here ain't cut out fer it."

"Those that're interested take a seat."

Half an hour later Trac felt the three would meet the job requirements. "Meet me in front of the General Store tomorrow morning at seven if you want to ride back with our crew. Otherwise...." He gave them directions to his place.

They shook hands and rejoined their friends. Glad to be finished, Trac took the back stairs up and found his room. The men would have the buying and loading done by now. Since Dan was in charge of supplies and they shared the room, Trac figured he had time for a hot bath.

Bathed, clean shaven, hair newly sheared Trac fell into the featherbed and slept like a baby. The fireplace cackled noisily but he never heard it or when Dan came in.

Trac was up early, fully rested and ready to head back.

It was a relief to know Janie's men would have some help as well. They were near worn out. At least Janie and the baby wouldn't be alone as much now...maybe Wilson would stay away, if it wasn't too late.

* * *

The return trip took longer than expected but by the end of the week, they'd had enough sun that the melted snow started to water the valleys below.

He brought back a Winchester model '73 carbine with a leather holster, exactly like the one he'd lost in the fire. He holstered the gun and tied it to his knee. It was good to have a Winchester again. He'd borrowed Emmett's gun but it didn't have the power he needed. They passed several elk standing in the tall trees. Spring would come early.

"Sure glad to get back to Wes' cookin." Cash laughed over the campfire. Those frijoles you made boss ain't near as good as when Wes makes 'em."

Trac smiled and served the beans, filling Cash's bowl higher than the rest. "And I'll be glad to get back to ranching instead of cooking." he replied.

The smell of fresh coffee boiling over the fire brought the rest of the men in for the night where, after eating their chow, they slept, some under the wagon, some under pallets they made on piles of pine branches. Riley brought out his banjo and played *Jeanie With the Light Brown Hair* and *Goober Peas*. Ranch hands weren't given much to singing but they enjoyed a cup of strong coffee and good music.

"You guys got any whiskey?" The new man, Pete, asked.

Trac remained quiet, staring into the fire, letting the men answer Pete's question. "Nope boss don't 'low no drinkin." Tom said, spitting tobacco juice into the fire and watching it hiss and kick up the fire for an instant.

Nothing else was said about it.

Joe, to Trac's way of thinking, appeared to be a decent man. He was young, single and seemed to have a good head about him. Most of the hands never asked questions when a new man came on; just waited to see if he could hold his own. If he didn't do his share, the men voted to send him packing. They took no chances on their own lives or on the rest of the crew's. Thieves, drunks and various other scalawags were not tolerated on the Cordera Ranch.

"Anybody needin' anything get in touch with me." Trac reminded his men. A series of nods and grunts around the fire indicated they understood. It was quiet for a long while. The moonlit sky sent strange shadows over the trees and rocks and seemed to mesmerize the men.

Trac took to his bed hoping Janie was all right. He remembered little Willa's birth and wondered if Janie remembered, too. That was as close as they'd ever been. That little baby girl was special to him, partly because he'd helped bring her into the world, partly because she belonged to Billy. A smile lit across his face in the dark before he fell asleep under the wagon.

After a few hours sleep, Trac called the men so they could finish the trip. The day was just dawning when they'd pulled up camp and headed down the road.

* * *

Louisa leaned down to look out her window, clear now of frost and by the new light saw the outline of the wagon before she heard the huge wood and iron wheels creaking on the muddy snow. She smiled as it rumbled past her place and headed down to the bunkhouse where the men would unload the food provisions and then over to the barn to unload the building supplies.

Fifteen minutes later, she heard Trac's familiar boot stomp at the door. "Everybody okay in here?" He whispered pushing the door open and shutting it quietly.

"All's well. Did you pass Mrs. Preston's place?"

"Yep, but it was dark."

"I do wish Janie would go to her mother's place. They need each other."

Trac's eyes narrowed. "What brought this up?" and took a chair.

"Oh nothing." She evaded.

"What's going on Louisa." He demanded over the rim of his coffee cup.

She turned and stoked the fire and Trac knew it was a stall tactic.

"Something I should know about?"

"No, no . . . it's just that Josiah Wilson is spouting to everyone that Janie said she'd marry him. Do you think he finally wore her down Trac? I mean if she won't go home to her mother and won't give up Billy's ranch, she may have given in."

Trac felt his heart turn to stone and said nothing for a long time, pondering the ifs and whether-or-nots.

"She could do worse."

"How can you say such a thing?" Louisa demanded.

"Meant what I said." He pressed his lips together and stretched out his legs toward the fire.

"Josiah Wilson good for Janie? Forgive me Trac, but I think he's a beast."

"Beast? I hardly think that's a proper term. Skunk's more like it."

"Then why did you let *him* have her?"

"I did not let anybody have anything, sis. Every time we try to talk we end up at a dead end. I don't know what else I can say to her."

"If you love her – like you say you do" and she was staring straight into his eyes, "then you would find the words. Why if I'd let Emmett take his sweet loving time, I'd be an old maid today."

"Emmett fell in love with you the moment he saw you Louisa. Everybody knows that."

"Is that so? Well, did you know that he was scared out of his mind to take a wife? What with his wandering spirit."

"No." Trac looked doubtful.

"He surely was. He told me so himself. Worried that once he'd started the whole thing it would never end. First the wife, then the cabin to build, and then any children that came along. He nearly talked himself out of marrying me at all."

"You don't say?" Trac was teasing now. "Emmett's got a good point there. It is an awful lot for a man to take on."

She ignored the big lump that was sitting in her chair and was glad when Grace woke for her feeding. She slipped into the bedroom careful not to wake Virginia and heard the front door close quietly just as the sun came up over the horizon.

Soon the sun was melting snow and shining through the glass, making everyone happy. Louisa was content enough to sit and knit near the low fire, with the sun beating in the windows. It was the first full day of it they'd had in a long time.

A knock at the door nearly frightened the life out of her. She'd fallen asleep in the rocker.

"Oh what a surprise. Janie. Josiah. Please come in. And how's little Willa?" She took the baby from Janie's arms.

"I asked Josiah to bring me on his way to Stonewall." Janie smiled with her mouth though not through her eyes.

Josiah Wilson looked uncomfortable, but was polite enough. "Ladies." He bowed out the door.

Louisa didn't know what to make of it. "Come, I'll get some tea. We're having beef and gravy on biscuits today. Hungry?"

"Starved. Thank you." Janie took Willa back in her arms and fed her while Louisa prepared tea.

Louisa hummed and prayed while her back was to Janie. Something was not right, but she didn't want to be nosey, so she waited.

"Suppose you've heard?" Janie said quietly.

Louisa's heart fell to the floor. *Then it was true. Janie had accepted Josiah's offer.*

"Heard what?" she asked.

"Josiah has told it outright that he and I, that he and I . . . "

"Are getting married." Louisa finished for her friend and knew her voice sounded unhappy.

"Yes. And I don't know what to do Louisa. Even my mother has sent word that she's coming to help me with the wedding dress, of all things."

"Oh." Louisa was confused. "Then you don't want to marry Josiah?"

"No, I do not." Janie stated fervently.

"Oh," Louisa sighed. "I am glad."

"You are? I thought — well, I thought that everyone would think me foolish to turn down a handsome offer to take over the ranch and build me a new house by the lake and raise Billy's daughter."

"You would be acting out of *gratefulness* I see it as an *honor* for Josiah Wilson to have that duty." Louisa said squaring her shoulders, a smile on her face.

Janie stared at her. "Then you're not angry with me?"

"Why, goodness no. Whatever gave you that idea?"

"Josiah said you would think less of me for turning down such a fine offer."

"Oh Janie. You've changed so." Louisa turned away, then after a few moments to collect her thoughts said, "In days past you were the brightest, happiest young woman I knew. I used to envy your ability to handle Billy. You loved him so and everyone knew it. And once you set your mind to something . . ." Louisa laughed, "Well, no one, and I mean no one, had better stand in your way."

"Was I really like that, Louisa? I can't remember."

"Janie, let me tell you." Louisa related a slew of funny tales.

"At the end, Janie sighed. "I'm just not the same anymore – I don't see how I ever can be again."

"Now don't go talking like that. You're a Cordera and you must be proud and strong. You are a fortunate woman to have loved a good man and be loved in return. Look, even little Willa is a gift from God to remember Billy by. And she looks so much like her pa."

Janie looked down at the child in her lap and hugged her closer. "Oh Louisa, I must confess, sometimes I see her as a burden. If she hadn't come along, I could have died and left this world. Now I'm...bound here."

"You're here because God wants it that way or you would have died and Willa with you. But you are alive, Janie. Alive. Start acting like it" Louisa was surprised at her own outburst, although it was not said unkindly, was perhaps not necessary.

Janie looked away as hot tears began to run down her cheeks. And then great gushing sobs tore from her body. Louisa jumped up and took Willa and laid her on Grace's pallet, then took Janie in her arms and let her cry it out.

"There. There. I was too harsh. You're just a soul here on earth. You're not expected to be an angel or anything close to it. You're flesh and blood and bone, like all of us and the Lord himself knows we're made of clay. But He loves us so. Even though Billy is not here, God loves you so Janie."

"I don't feel it." She whimpered into her hands. "I don't feel God loves me at all."

"Of course you don't, you're grieving for Billy. There are people in this world who need you. Look for them Janie. Look for them."

The soothing words encouraged Janie's heart deep in a place she didn't think still existed. She did feel something. A tiny grain of hope.

"How can we undo all that Josiah has set in motion?" Janie wiped the tears from her face, tired of crying. "Even Reverend Dunham paid me a visit after Josiah told him we were getting married."

"Who else knows?" Louisa pulled up a chair at the table and Janie joined her.

"My mother, as you know, and Cash asked me when he came to feed the animals. I am guessing everyone in the county must know by now." Janie moaned. "With spring coming and everyone looking for set-tos and parties, they will be thinking . . ."

"The news got around once and it can get around again." Louisa said firmly, tapping her fingers on the table. "We'll start the truth and hope it gets around the same way the lies got around. If I'm not mistaken he told Trac some time ago that you were getting married."

"He did?" Janie's eyes grew large.

"If my memory serves me correctly, I do believe it was a couple of months ago."

"He's been telling people for some time now. What a mess." Janie groaned.

"If the warmer weather holds, let's try to get to church on Sunday. We'll start with the Reverend and the fine people there and see if they can carry the truth as quickly as they can carry other tales."

Janie laughed out loud. "You are so practical Louisa."

For the next hour they exchanged ideas on how to back out of an engagement that never was in the first place.

Spring would be here in a couple of months, the mountain-fresh water would soon be running strong and the children would be able to play outdoors again.

Suddenly the door swung open and a huge body stepped in. With the sun behind it was hard to tell who. "How're my girls." Trac stomped his feet, then stopped short when he found himself standing face to face with Janie.

"Janie." His voice betrayed him. "Didn't know you were here. Where's Josiah?"

Janie sent him a look and groaned. Even Trac thought it too.

He looked at his sister. What had he done now?

"I think we'd better tell him." Louisa said and turned to Janie.

Janie stuttered out, "Josiah and I are *not* getting married."

"I heard the opposite was true."

"What you heard was wrong." Janie reiterated solemnly.

"So what're all the long faces for?" Trac felt his heart race.

"Seems that Mr. Wilson has told the entire county, including Janie's mother and Reverend Dunham otherwise." Louisa explained.

"I see." Trac said quietly as he turned his back to fill the bowl with the pitcher, a smile on his face. "I'll wash up."

Louisa began to lay out dinner.

Chapter 31

After supper the women cleaned up. "I promised to read to the girls tonight." She started for the stack of books on the shelf.

"I'll read to the girls." Trac announced.

Louisa smiled, "You're sure."

"Sure enough to let you two go off to the bedroom and have a cup of tea – if you've a mind to."

"Shall we have a tea party?" Louisa asked Janie as she curt-seyed, holding her skirts out to the side.

Janie smiled.

"Virginia, be a good girl and bring Uncle Trac a couple blan-kets from your mother's room. We'll be sitting on the floor. Safer that way." He smiled as she ran off.

Trac settled the quilts on the floor and sat, settled Virginia next to him, careful for her arm. "Bring Grace." Louisa put Grace on her brother's left knee. "Okay bring Willa." He looked at Janie.

"Are you sure?" She asked. At his nod she picked up the fussy Willa and set her on Trac's right arm.

"Now ladies off to your tea party," He laughed. "But I assure I won't be able to withstand this position long, so come when I call."

Trac had smelled Janie's fresh-washed hair as she settled Willa into his arm. He wanted to reach out and touch it's dark brown softness. Propriety forbid him to do so in company, but one of these days . . .

He was waxing foolish tonight, perhaps because Janie had turned down the good Josiah Wilson.

Grace wiggled to be free so Trac placed her belly-down on the quilt. She was content immediately. He began to read letting the eldest turn the pages. One book, then another. Virginia's lips moved with each word. She'd memorized every word.

Some time later, not hearing a peep, Louisa cracked the door for a look. The books had been forsaken and Trac was making up stories as he went along. Virginia listened, intrigue written all over her face, while Grace played with a corner of the quilt. Willa, still on Trac's arm, had fallen asleep. What a portrait they made.

Janie came for a look, unable to believe he could entertain three little ones for that long. Something in Janie's heart healed. Trac Gage Cordera could no more have been responsible for Billy's death than she could have. He had loved Billy as much as she had. Why hadn't she seen it before?

Her conscience was struck with unbelief. Why had she been so bitter for so long? So hateful. So willing to take vengeance out on Trac because he'd made the bet?

Then she answered her own question. *Because he was safe.*

The women, glad to have quiet with no interruptions, did not disturb the children and went back to their conversation, keeping the door slightly ajar.

Half an hour passed when they heard a quiet knock. "Ladies, you may come out now." Trac announced triumphantly. "The girls are asleep, all of them in the wrong places, but they are asleep."

Virginia and Grace were snuggled together on the quilt and Willa had been placed in Grace's cradle. Tiptoeing about, the mothers checked on their children and whispered, "How did you do that?"

"Easy enough. I told Virginia I"d take her out to play tomorrow if she could get Grace to sleep and Willa was easy enough to rock. It can be done ladies." He bowed, pulled on his boots, duster and Stetson and slipped out the door, a better man having bested the ladies at their own game.

Conversation and mending continued on into the evening. Louisa noted the slight smile that rested on Janie's face.

Chapter 32

The extra hands on board helped the last of the winter months go quickly. It was time for spring roundup and church picnics. The women had spent hours sewing trousers and work shirts for the men who'd lost everything in the fire. Janie had spent the last few weeks at Louisa's cabin. That Singer sewing machine pedal had run til the wee hours many an evening.

Trac barely had time to catch up on chores once roundup and counting time arrived. They took advantage of every half-warm day. With three hundred acres to tend to Trac was glad for every cowboy on the ranch.

Wes's work increased with the extra mouths to feed, since the regulars had returned from spending the winter with their families, not to mention he was busier than a bee gathering honey, buzzing around picking up supplies and getting seeds for spring planting.

"Got any dried apples left?" Trac called out to his cook the next morning.

"Boss, there's barely enough time to get the plates rinsed out before another batch of stinkin', hungry men are back again for another meal." He wiped the sweat from his creased forehead.

"You do look worse for the wear." He shot back. "Looks like you need some time off."

"Fact is, I was thinkin' the same thing myself just yesterday. But been so busy ain't had time to ask yet. What about it? Say this Sunday? Got something I gotta tend to." Wes added importantly.

Trac noticed a slight twinkle in his blue eyes. "Anything you want to share with us?"

"Nope."

Trac sidled closer to Wes and whispered, "Lady?"

Wes started to deny, then turned sheepish eyes up and stopped his work. "Matter of fact . . ."

"You've earned a day off. Take tomorrow and half the next day. I'll get Louisa to come down and cook us something. But day after tomorrow be back in time to feed the crew for suppertime."

"You bet." Wes' face lit up.

"Besides, we'll be needin' some of that apple pie I spoke about earlier."

Wes' eyes narrowed, then he smiled. "Sure enough Boss, day after tomorrow. Be the best pie you ever 'et."

Trac pushed his hat back. "Lucky man" he mumbled and couldn't help wondering when he'd had the time to court. He was nearing fifty years old, had ridden the range since he was eight and knew everything there was to know about ranching. Took the Cook's job after he'd been thrown from his horse, injuring his back, when he and a buffalo met head-on.

Twice Trac gazed up at the white clouds in the bright blue sky, it looked to be a good day. Dust rose from the road. Someone was coming. He squinted his eyes and saw immediately it was Emmett. It was Monday morning and he was looking mighty happy sitting atop his horse. He pulled a small wagon.

"Welcome back, man." Trac shouted as he met him on the road.

"The place has changed." Emmett said as he looked out over the horizon. "New bunkhouse?"

"Yep, other one burned down."

He nodded.

"Better get on inside. There are some gals waiting for you in there." Trac slapped his hat on his thigh and followed.

Emmett's tan face and white teeth beamed with delight.

"I'll bring your trunk in unless it's full of gold nuggets, then you can carry it yourself." Trac dropped to the ground.

"Nope. Gold's hidden. Too many roadside robberies." He said knowingly, then "I need to see my wife and my girls."

Emmett walked right in and Trac heard Louisa's scream. Trac followed with a carpetbag, set it inside and shut the door. Louisa was swinging in Emmett's arms, her long skirt trailing out behind her like a ship's sail. He waited a minute and then brought in more parcels.

Janie stood away, her hands wiping a dish, with a wistful look. She looked up and found Trac's gaze settled on her face. Her eyes dropped, and she turned away, ashamed she'd been so clearly envying Louisa's return of her husband.

Trac had not missed the longing look in her dark eyes. He, too, longed to take Janie in his arms and swing her around until she screamed with joy at seeing him. He retrieved two more trunks and made himself scarce. "No sense in heart-hurtin' yourself." He mumbled kicking up dust with his worn cowboy boots.

Later, Janie found him down at the barn. Trac was surprised when Dan had come telling him Janie wanted to see him. She'd walked up, twisting her apron in her hands. "Something on your mind?" He kept working. Her proximity in the small space made him sweat.

"I was wondering if you'd mind taking me and Willa home?" She stopped, looking back at the house. "You know....with Emmett home and everything . . ." her voice dropped away.

"Won't be until near dark. Got to get things ready for the morning. We're branding tomorrow."

"Yes, I know. I'm sorry to be a bother."

"You're not a bother, Janie." Trac's heard the tiredness in his own voice. When he looked up again, he saw her walking briskly back to the house.

Tomorrow was one of their busiest days of the year. Since the cattle had been rounded up and separated, they'd be branding for two, maybe three days without any sleep. It was a hot, sweaty, dirty, tiring job. He was grateful for the extra men this year. His back had been giving him trouble lately especially in the saddle.

It was near impossible not to end up with back trouble when a man spent so much time on a horse riding over the rough terrain. Hours later Trac, ready for tomorrow, headed up to the ranch house. The sun was already settling over the landscape. He needed to get Janie home and hit the sack. Dawn had come far too quick these last few weeks.

Janie washed up Emmett's dishes and excused herself to the bedroom to feed Willa, but the time couldn't move along fast enough to suit her. Emmett and Louisa were leaning into each other talking in low tones and laughing quietly exchanging looks Janie could not abide. She took Willa for a walk outdoors to enjoy the sun and get away from the lovers for awhile . . . give them a chance to—suddenly she missed Billy. Had almost forgotten what it was like to rest in his arms, to feel his touch, to know she was loved. Only ten months. That's all they had. It seemed like she was never married sometimes and feared she'd forget what Billy's face looked like.

She needed someone. Now. She'd take Willa to see her grand-mother. Mrs. Preston had spent so little time with her grandchild, mostly because of winter. Janie knew there was another reason; she avoided her mother — her mother had the most irritating habit of thinking she had the answer for every emotion Janie suffered. The reason Janie preferred Louisa's company. If she was quiet, her mother would tell her to take a walk; if she was staring at her needlework, she'd suggest doing something new and had even gone so far as to suggest she should think about marrying again soon. . . for Willa's sake, of course. Not to mention the fact she was barely on speaking terms with her mother because she had refused Josiah Wilson's 'perfectly good offer.' Janie loved her mother dearly but could not take the constant barrage of advice.

She'd heard Reverend Dunham preach more than once about accepting your lot in life; but for some reason she could not get it into her head that she still had a life worth living. How did anyone know what she was feeling or thinking?

Even Josiah Wilson avoided her since the truth was finally known that they were never betrothed.

Willa, asleep on her shoulder became heavy. At nearly five months she was a dark-haired chubby angel. Janie kissed the top of her soft curls and whispered. "Your daddy would have loved you so much." Tears scalded bitter paths down her dusty face and fell off her cheeks wetting Willa's hair.

Behind her she heard the wagon. Swiping her hands across her eyes, she lifted the corner of her apron to remove any silly traces, while balancing her sleeping child on one arm.

"Ready?"

"Yes." She avoided Trac's gaze. He had been so quiet and tired lately that they'd barely spoken. And now that Emmett was back he'd not been up at the ranch, then reminded herself that he was in a hurry. "I'll run in and get our things." She said and started walking...

"Bring Willa to me." He looked down at her from the wagon seat. "I'll hold her unless you need help with your bundles."

Janie hurried back and handed her sleeping baby upward. Trac's tanned hands covered hers for a moment sending shivers up her arm as he gently settled the baby in his lap. Amazingly she did not wake. Their eyes met for the smallest of moments and he saw the old sadness in her brown eyes. Would it ever go away? Trac wondered, as he looked out over the setting sun.

Janie tossed several small bundles in the back of the wagon, held up her skirts with one hand and grabbed Trac's hand with the other. Trac noticed her worn shoes. He adjusted the baby to his left arm and with his right hand hauled her up and across his feet to her seat. She settled as far away from him as the railing would allow. He handed Willa to her mother.

"She's getting a mite heavy." Though tired, he tried to be friendly. Janie smiled but said nothing.

"Won't be long and she'll be bigger than you." He added and slapped the reins. It was getting dark fast.

They traveled in silence, the familiar night sounds echoing in their ears. The smell of pine, the rush of blowing bramble weed, even the sound of the night birds, seemed so strange after the months of white blizzard. "Nice night."

"Yes it is." She sighed.

"We're heading into town after the branding is done. Need anything?"

"I'll make a list."

"Good. Better add a pair of shoes to that list," he said quietly, lest she get huffy with him for noticing.

She turned her head, said nothing, a wistful look pervading her emotions. Again. Sometimes he wanted to shake her and tell her to come out it; sometimes he wanted to kiss her until she melted in his arms.

The dark cabin came slowly into view, silhouetted in the sky. "I'll get the lamps lit." He pulled the wagon to a stop and jumped down.

She obeyed like a child and before long, there was a small fire in the grate to ward off the evening chill. Willa was settled into her cradle.

"Paper?" he asked, rubbing his aching hands together.

"Paper?"

"For your shoe size."

"Oh." Her embarrassed flush did nothing to waylay him. She handed him her shoe.

"Won't do."

"Why not?"

"Put your foot here. Shoe size is not determined by shoes, but by feet." Janie could see he was slightly irritated.

She did as he said and removed her shoe and placed her black-stockinged foot on the paper. She gasped as Trac took hold of her ankle, pressed her foot to the paper, then traced her entire foot, heels, instep and each toe. When he released her she stepped backward and nearly fell into the rocking chair.

"Whoa." He grabbed her arm as he raised to his full height in a quick move. She pulled free of him immediately and put as much space as she could between them, fleeing behind the table as though a wolf were chasing her.

He smiled, maybe because he was too tired or because he found the look on her face amusing. Her big eyes stared out from beneath her wind-blown hair. She was so vulnerable, he hated to leave her alone in the cabin. And it wasn't like the old Janie to be afraid of anything.

"You sure you'll be all right?"

"What's so funny?"

"Nothing. Nothing." But he couldn't help smiling again.

"Then why are you laughing."

"I'm not laughing, I'm smiling."

"Then what're you smiling for?"

"Are you afraid of me Janie?" he asked with a glint in his eye.

"I most certainly am not." She huffed.

"Then why are you hiding behind that table?"

"Oh." She appeared to relax and walked around to the side, but he still noticed she gripped the chair back.

"Afraid of your feelings?"

She crossed her arms over and stalked away, threw another small log on the fire and ignored his question.

"Just asking. You need anything?"

"No, I won't be needing anything."

"It's not good for you two to be here alone." He added for the hundredth time.

"I'm fine. Besides, it's none of your business," she sputtered and busied herself rearranging dishes on the shelf.

"Well, then, guess I'll go."

"Good evening." She gave him her back, lifted her chin and glanced over her shoulder to see where he was at.

He walked out into the darkness and put the latch in place. His men would be there to feed and water the stock in the morning. After that they would be busy for several days. He hated leaving her there. One of these days he was going to give her a good talking to and if that didn't work, he'd put her over his knee. He untied his Winchester from his leg so he could stretch his aching muscles, a full-faced smile on his face as he pulled slowly away.

Chapter 33

At dawn the next morning branding began in earnest. Each man pulled his own weight. Just keeping the fires hot enough took a lot of energy. Trac worked round the clock with half his crew while the other half saw to the other daily duties that had to be done. The men slept in four-hour shifts. By the third day he was tired and not thinking clearly. He'd just roped a steer and was about to set her down when he lurched his back. Immediately his muscles went into a spasm and he found himself writhing on the ground.

"Boss?"

After a few minutes of burning, searing pain, he squeezed the words from clenched teeth. "Sprained my back and think I cracked a couple ribs." He drew in what little breath he could. "Hard to breathe."

The men finished what he'd started and Wes leaned over him, "It's bad boss?"

"It's bad, Wes. Get Dan and Riley. They can heft me up. Maybe if I stand."

"I'll help ya. Don't worry just take my arm."

Trac looked at Wes and not wanting to insult him, allowed Wes to help him to his feet. He nearly cried out at the pain and could not stand up straight.

"Better get you down to the bunkhouse. Wes walked him down slowly. Trac was astounded at the powerful muscles in his arms. Wes was a strong man, even though his back wasn't what it used to be.

Trac tried to talk but air would not fill his lungs. His breath was pulled in small amounts and with great difficulty. "Thanks Wes, didn't think I could make it." A puff of air escaped from his lungs as he slowly eased back on the bed.

"Don't you worry none. We'll take care of everything just like always. I'll go up and help out."

"Wes, I could use a cup of strong coffee."

"Sure boss. Wes hurried off and was back in five minutes, a cup of steaming coffee and a biscuit with a wad of butter, stood on the makeshift table next to Trac's bed. Next thing he knew Wes pulled off his boots.

"Man cain't rest with his boots on." He said.

"Thanks buddy, I'll try to relax, see if I can't get this twisted muscle back to working." He winced as he tried to move.

"If'n you got that trouble and a couple o'cracked ribs to go along with it, you ain't moving for awhile. Sit tight. It's the last day. Job's almost done."

Wes was out the door and Trac knew he'd do the job, even with a bad back.

No matter which way he turned he was helpless. He wished he'd asked Wes to help him out of his dusty chaps and shirt too. He lay on a clean bed with dust all over him and tried to sleep. It was impossible. Here he lay like an injured bird. Four of the men came in for their sleep shift and moved quietly, most of them too tired to talk anyway. He heard water splashing in the wash bowl, the wet towel as it thumped against the wall when one of the men tossed it in the direction of the peg.

All during the night men would come in, wash, eat, sleep, and get up and back to work. Louisa had come down with some laudanum left over from Virginia's broken arm and he'd known his sister was helping Wes with the cooking. He must have slept a week, at least that's what it felt like. Unshaven, unwashed, and mean as a rabid dog, he'd had about enough laying about.

He found he could move a bit and tried sitting up. It took ten minutes, groaning like a stuck pig the whole time. He managed to get those chaps off and stand up long enough to wash up and shave. Every move took all the energy he could muster. Finally, he called out to Wes, who called the men together. He paid them and gave them Saturday off. They'd worked hard, finished a day early, and he was in no mood to have them waiting around for him to get better. "Go on into town, pick up supplies, and be sure you're back here for the church picnic on Sunday."

"Picnic." The men grumbled.

"Yep, won't hurt any of you to sit through a church service once a year, besides there's going to be some of the best food you'll ever eat this side of the Mississippi. We'll pull out at eight after chores."

The men looked sideways at each other, but agreed after Trac added. "Prettiest girls this side of the fault line, too."

That changed their minds, at least the single ones. The married ones were mostly into the idea there would be good food and plenty of it.

Pretty soon he heard a comment or two about getting a new shirt or pair of boots while they were in Stonewall. Not much to pick from, but there was no time to go to Helena in one day. Some of the guys talked about tuning up their fiddles and banjos.

Louisa had run down when she could to see if she could help him by rubbing his back with some concoction she'd made and performing such other medicinal experiments she'd heard about from her lady friends. Thus far nothing had worked and Trac sensed he was interrupting her time with Emmett and the girls, so he feigned being better when she was around, practicing sitting up and standing when he could manage it.

He'd done it all right, too, even though it had nearly killed him to do it. But he was determined not to be a bed bug and slowly, moving inch by inch, brought himself to his feet several times. Couldn't walk much but he could stand. A couple more days and he would walk if he worked at it. He didn't want to miss the church picnic, either. Too much good food. And Janie would be there.

The ranch was quiet on Saturday. All the men were gone and even Louisa hadn't showed up. He knew she was preparing cakes and pies. Fried chicken was on the menu because he'd heard the ruckus down at the hen house. Which reminded him he'd better try to get up again.

He was just easing his feet down over the side of the bed, exquisite pain nearly causing him to groan aloud. In a sitting position he was just gaining his legs when his door flew open and Janie walked through.

Trac sat back down again, a puff of air escaping from his lungs. "Scared the life out of me." He snapped. "Why didn't you yell or something?" He gritted out.

"Sorry, I brought your dinner."

"Where's Louisa?"

"She's gone to town with Emmett and the girls. They left early this morning."

"She didn't tell me." He tried to stretch his legs out and then remembered he was sitting in his long underwear and pulled a blanket over his legs.

"Brought you some soup. Louisa made it before she left."

"I see." He took the bowl and their knuckles touched. She pulled back, offered him the spoon and pulled up a chair, then went out to the cook stove.

"Coffee?" She tossed the words over her shoulder.

"Yes."

She set it down on the small table and turned to leave.

"Sit down yourself." He invited, rubbing his dark chin.

"Willa is up at the house."

"Go get her. I could use some company." He ordered.

She jumped up, her mouth thinned in frustration at being bossed around, but she was back in a few minutes.

"Say there." He chucked the baby's chin and she giggled, her brown eyes bright. "She sure is pretty."

Janie seemed pleased at the compliment.

"Just like her mother..." Trac added, sneaking a sideways glance at Janie.

Janie ignored his comment.

"You need a bath, Trac Cordera." She said smartly.

"Is that so? Well, why don't you just tell me how I'm going to get one, when I can't do anything more than stand."

"If you can stand, you can walk." She obviously felt no pity.

He finished his soup, told her to turn her back, and moaned several times getting his trousers on. He stood very slowly, hand on the bedpost for strength, and told her she could turn around. "I'm up. Now what?"

His challenging tone set her determination even more.

"I'll help you to the washtub." She set Willa on the floor with a wooden spoon to keep her busy and came up next to him and positioned her feet firmly. He put his long arm around her shoulder smiling. How was she, little as she was, going to help him?

But help him she did and finally they were standing near the washtub, his forehead in a sweat.

"You suggesting I just jump in there?"

"I'll fill the tub, you can wash. Willa and I will head back up to the house."

She warmed water and filled the tub. Trac watched her small frame make half a dozen trips with the bucket. It was good to see her so full of purpose.

When she was done, she pulled a chair next to the bath, looped a towel over his shoulder, tossed in a bar of lye soap and picked up Willa. "We'll be back in an hour or so."

"Knock before you come in this time." He called over his shoulder.

She ignored his crankiness, which made him more ill-tempered.

It took a full ten agonizing minutes to get his clothes off, another ten to get his legs into the tub and a couple more to crouch down enough to get himself wet. Grunts and groans escaped his lips and he was glad to be alone in his misery.

He reached for the tin cup that hung on the side of the large wooden tub and poured water over his head. Soaped up and rinsed. What a wonderful sensation. He was clean again. After a good soak, he was just about to raise himself up, when he heard the knock and the squeak of the door.

"I'm not done yet."

"Well, goodness knows, you've had almost two hours." Janie called out.

"So? I'll be out in a few minutes. Take a walk." He suggested through thin lips.

His surly attitude was uncharacteristic of the gentle Trac she knew. He really must be hurting. Determined to be a little more helpful she answered sweetly. "We'll be back in an hour then."

"It won't take *that* long." He complained but she ignored him again.

Just to be sure, she and Willa took an extra long walk. The day was beautiful and the wind in her hair felt glorious, not to mention that Willa loved being outdoors. Like her father. Truth was, Janie would be glad when Willa could walk.

By the time Janie returned it was late afternoon and her arms were wore out from carrying Willa. Too bad Trac couldn't take a walk and dry his hair, she thought wistfully. It would do him good. And, when she thought about it...she wanted companionship. Even if he was grumpy.

She knocked again.

"Come in." He called, some of the tension having left, his tone of voice more agreeable.

She found him sitting on the chair next to the bath, fully dressed, hair brushed back, although not combed through, and looking quite pleased with himself.

"You did it." She smiled.

"Sure did. It feels good to be clean. Would you mind changing the sheets on the bed?"

When she agreed, he told her, "I'll take Willa."

She settled her squirming body on his lap and she cried. Loud. "What's wrong?" he looked to Janie.

"She's getting older and she doesn't remember you holding her when she was tiny." She explained. "Talk to her, I'll move away. When she can't see me, she'll be all right."

"Hey there little gal. Don't get too busy now. Your Uncle Trac can't take too much movement."

"You're not her uncle." Janie called over her shoulder, as she put fresh bedding on Trac's bed.

"Next best thing." He answered back.

"A father would be the *next best thing,*" she shot back, hands on her hips.

He smiled. *"Your mama's one fine woman."* He said to Willa and heard Janie spit out "What did you say?"

He ignored her.

"Bed's made. Need help getting back?" She took Willa and set her on the floor where she happily clapped her chubby hands.

"I'm pretty stiff yet. Back muscle is better but the ribs...it's hard to pull myself up. This is making me crazy Janie." He was serious now.

She understood his need to be about his business and actually felt sorry for him.

He placed his hands on the seat of the chair and began to lift himself, groans escaping from between clenched teeth. Janie placed herself underneath his arm and helped him carry his weight back to the bed.

"Lay on your stomach." She ordered and then went to the cook's cabinet.

"Why. What're you doing?"

"Getting some lard."

"What for?" he inquired as he slowly turned his body over, his face breaking out in a sweat.

"You're sweating already."

"I told you it hurts like crazy." He was raising his voice again.

"You don't have to get puffed up. Pull up your shirt and I'll put some of this on."

"I can't pull up my shirt. It would kill me to reach around."

"Very well." She grabbed two handfuls of shirt and jerked it up until his muscled back was exposed, then began to rub the lard up and down his spine. It hurt at first, then slowly she began to push harder. His muscles screamed for mercy, but he held himself in check. After awhile her ministrations actually began to relax his body.

"Willa's being awful good over there. Haven't heard a peep from her." He said sleepily.

"She's a good child. Playing with that little bird Billy whittled. She loves that bird."

"Like her daddy." He said quietly.

The poignant moment of understanding was nearly her undoing. She'd worked so hard to be stronger, but there were times . . . times when she just wanted to crumble into the earth with loneliness.

She choked back tears and rubbed Trac's back harder.

"Whoa, I think I've had enough."

"Okay." She wiped her hands on a towel, picked up Willa and made a quick exit, throwing over her shoulder, "I hope you sleep well." He heard the bunkhouse door shut with a thud.

"Thanks." He yelled. Oddly enough his body did feel relaxed. With a great amount of effort he turned onto his back and fell asleep thinking how wonderful a bath and clean bed were and wishing he hadn't been so irritable with Janie.

Chapter 34

"**S**poiled, that's what he is. Thinks he's everybody's boss." Janie sputtered aloud to her daughter whose smile widened. That's when she saw it. "A tooth, and so early, Willa." She whispered and stopped to peep into her mouth.

Suddenly tears popped into her eyes as her steps hit the ground hard. She wondered what Billy would have said. She wished they could hurry home and show Willa's father her new tooth. Oh, she was so confused, so lonely. Maybe she should marry Josiah Wilson and have a home. Surely he would grow accustomed to Willa soon enough, while she was still small and knew no other man as her father. And if she tried really hard to be a good wife, she might even make Josiah happy.

Deep in thought, she heard someone and looked up. Josiah Wilson riding up to Louisa's house that very minute. She hurried up the hill.

"Mrs. Cordera." He greeted formally and stepped down looking dapper in a navy pin-striped suit with knee-high black boots. "I've come to give you the good news." He removed his hat and smoothed his hair.

Janie shaded her eyes to look up. He cut a fine figure. A tall man, his stance confident, the sun glowing behind him. "What news."

"I'm to be president of Montana Bank and Trust." He said proudly, looking off into the distance, waiting for her response.

"I'm happy for you Josiah." She said softly.

"Please, from now on refer to me as Mr. Wilson." Then added quickly, "if you don't mind. It's only proper for a man in my position to be addressed as such."

"Of course." She acquiesced quietly. "It is quite a thing to become president – of anything." She agreed.

"It is at that, isn't it?"

Janie noticed he hadn't addressed or even looked at Willa.

"Would you care to come in for coffee...*Mr. Wilson*."

He pulled out a gold watch from his pocket and checked it. It glinted in the sun and Willa turned her face. "I do believe I have the time." He removed his riding gloves and slapped the dust against the post and followed her in.

He pulled a chair from the table and seated himself while Janie put Willa in the cradle for her nap, then set about to pour from the tin coffee pot.

"I came by not only to tell you of my good fortune, but to ask if you might attend the church picnic with me on Sunday."

Caught off guard and somewhat impressed by Josiah's new position, she accepted.

"Good, then. I shall pick you up in my new conveyance. I won't tell you what it is – you'll have to wait to see it, but I guarantee you will enjoy being seen with me."

"Oh." Janie wondered immediately if she'd done the right thing. He was so pompous. But she was just so lonely.

With a new lilt in his step and a new hat on his head he quit the cabin, calling out, "I'll be stopping early. Won't want to be late. It doesn't set well for someone in my position to be late. I'll arrive precisely at eight."

She nodded and he hurried off importantly, leaving in her wake a strong fragrance of cologne water. Her nose twitched and she sneezed.

It had only been recently that the rumors about her and Josiah Wilson had finally died down and now they would all start again. She doubted she could put them to rest after showing up at the picnic with him.

"Oh dear, Willa, what have I done?" She looked down at her sleeping child. She must never let anything ever come between her and her daughter. Determined to keep proper distance while attending the picnic with Josiah, she made plans to be reserved with him, polite but not too much.

* * *

Trac began to raise himself from his bed and try to walk. Every breath hurt, but he pushed himself. Ever since Janie had rubbed his back with that lard, he'd felt some relief and could actually move about quite freely, but not for too long.

A walk down to the creek behind the house on a warm, sunny afternoon did him good. An hour sitting on the lush green banks gave him time to think. The creek was at full capacity with the spring thaw and it flowed with an intensity he'd hardly noticed before now.

Someday he hoped to build a small bridge across the creek. A sullen thought passed through him then. Who would he bring here to walk across it? To enjoy it? He wanted it to be Janie but a man could hardly *make* a woman love him if she hated him.

Stiff from sitting on the damp ground, he stood and let the surge of rushing water hitting the rocks spray him until he was good and wet. It felt good. Only then did he realize how weary he was from this past year's troubles.

"Lord, I'm only a man." He spoke aloud, then turned slowly, and made his way back to his bed, too exhausted to do anything else.

The day of the picnic arrived warm and bright. Emmett and Louisa's house was full to overflowing with joy and so many baked dishes, Trac could hardly stand the smell. Starved, for Wes had gone early saying he had errands, he'd settled for a cup of coffee as breakfast. Trac knew for certain now since Wes had confirmed it this afternoon, he was seeing Mrs. Preston, Janie's mother. Mrs. Preston, a proper woman from back east, and Wes a seasoned cowboy turned cook. It was rather a strange match, but then God has his ways. Trac was glad for Wes.

Emmett was home for Louisa, Wes was courting. And he'd heard from his sister about Wilson's new position and that Janie had reluctantly agreed to attend with him. Maybe he should have called on Miss Delaney Denton. He'd been so determined not to be caught by a woman, he'd probably ruined his chances with Miss Denton or any other woman in Stonewall.

He made the walk up the hill, out of breath, but stronger and found Emmett and his family packing the wagon with the baskets of fried chicken, potatoes for baking over the fire, and assorted pies, cakes and pickled eggs, his favorite. Next came the straw and the quilts on top. He couldn't even help with that so he stood aside. Trac watched as Josiah Wilson came in his shiny new black Phaeton, complete with a gold stripe.

Time after time he had to deal with his aching heart watching Janie go with Josiah Wilson. He wanted to punch the man in the face. Truth, he was disappointed that Janie had accepted his offer. Was she so lost she couldn't see the man behind the clothes? He dreaded the hours ahead knowing he'd have to watch Wilson strutting around with Janie on his arm the entire afternoon.

Trac decided to follow along on his horse at a much slower pace. He knew Job sensed his need. Now that he was healing, he didn't want to reinjure the muscles in his back or dislodge those broken rib bones. It was too long and too painful a process to live over again.

When the picnic was over, folks would go back to their work, for the warm months were times that had to be embraced before a vicious Montana winter hit them again. And he fully intended to throw himself into his work and try to forget Janie Cordera and everything that happened. Strange, she possessed his last name but she wasn't his.

The ride was slow but Trac used the time to gaze out over the land. It had been so long since he'd been to the back end of the property, he made the effort to ride out there on the way. The Red Canyon River ran on the edge of his and Billy's property. That, along with the creek, had made it a prime piece and he was grateful when he realized how his father and Billy's father had been so wise in their choice. The valley had excellent grassland, plenty of wooded area, the creek and the river. He was proud to own it.

Perhaps, he thought, as he turned Job's head, it was time to do some building himself. Maybe take a wife. He'd had plenty of time to think about it. And he was nearing thirty.

His men came clean and dressed. The church was full and spirits were high as the preacher, glad to have so many ears, talked about loving their neighbor. Then it was time to eat.

Soon he could hear children yelling and see them playing with a stick and a ball, boys playing mumbelty-peg and the girls whispering shyly behind their hands as they cheered. A banjo and drums were pounding out *Camptown Races* and a few hearty souls sang loudly.

The sky was a deep blue, with soft white clouds floating aimlessly, which added to the excitement. Dismounting easy-like, Trac tied Job to a tree branch and rubbed him down slowly, fed him a carrot he'd carried along.

Settling his Stetson on his head, and hardening his heart, he walked into the crowd. He saw mothers of single daughters turn to whisper to each other. He knew any unattached man was fair game, especially at church socials, which were few and far between. Where else could a young woman meet a man?

Joseph, his new crewman, and single was circled by two mothers, each with a pretty daughter. He smiled. Poor man would be hard-put to get away from that entanglement.

It wasn't long before Mrs. Winton, Mrs. Laban, and Mrs. Quigly had pulled him into their mother's circle. He held a plate overflowing with fried chicken, sweet potatoes, corn and sweet bread. Seating himself quickly on one of the benches before he dropped the whole affair he found himself next to Mrs. Laban's daughter. He couldn't remember her name, so tipped his head and laid his hat on the bench. He was brought up to remember his manners. You greeted each one you met and you never ate with your hat on unless you were out on the range with the men.

"Mr. Cordera." The sweet voice spoke from his right.

He looked into a pair of handsome green eyes. Her light brown hair was done in a figure eight at the back of her head. He noticed when she reached down for something on the ground.

"Why yes." He stumbled over the words after swallowing. He couldn't remember her name.

""It's Abilene. Abilene Laban." She saw his trouble.

"Of course, Miss Laban. I don't get into town much."

"I have seen you in the General Store sometimes. I make lace trappings for the ladies' dresses and sell them….among other items." Her voice held a cultured tone.

Trac nodded and couldn't think of a thing to say about lace trappings…and other things, so he took a big bite of food.

She ate with ladylike slowness and he thought it best to pace himself to match her speed. He had gotten used to gulping food down on the trail or in his office. The straw hat she wore had brown ribbons that blew in the wind, and flowers that matched her brown print dress. She smelled nice, too. He was glad he'd gotten in the rushing creek and bathed just this morning. He'd found being in the water soothing to his muscles.

"You are quite handsome, Mr. Cordera. All the girls are looking this way. I surmise they envy me a great deal, visiting with you."

Trac stopped chewing and looked at her. "You speak plainly Miss Laban."

"That's what folks say. I hardly think a conversation worth it's while if folks don't speak plainly."

"My thoughts exactly. Except I'm not too good at doing the talking. I'd rather hear other folks talk than hear myself talk."

"Men usually don't care for conversation." She stated matter-of-factly.

This was a mature young woman sitting next to him and he began to relax.

"You are right about that ma'am."

"Oh please do not address me as ma'am. That's reserved for older women. It sounds so stuffy."

"Miss Laban, then?"

""Miss Laban is fine. Abilene is better." She whispered.

"Abilene." He tried her name on his tongue.

"Well, Mr. Cordera. My father is giving me the look. He prefers I not spend the entire time with one gentleman. He wishes me to 'make the rounds.'

Trac nodded in understanding.

"Besides..." she leaned closer, "There are several women eyeing you wishing to be in my enviable position. And I am not one to hinder Providence." She smiled and was gone.

Trac pulled in a deep breath and gulped down some lemonade. He liked Miss Laban. She was proper, said what she meant, and was beautiful besides. He pledged to find her again before the day was over. In the meantime, three lovely pink, blue, and yellow dresses were headed his way. Two brown-haired ladies and one redhead. Two tall, one very tiny. He finished gulping down the last of the chicken and sweet potatoes before he had to speak politely.

Olivia Riley was among the three. He'd dealt with her at the General Store and found her to be a bit high-minded, but easy enough to talk to. The other two only looked at him through lowered lashes, as though they wanted to say something, but they never did. In a few minutes another well-dressed man walked by and Trac watched the girls eyeing him.

Then he saw Janie. On Josiah Wilson's arm. He looked away but his eyes carried themselves back of their own accord. She was actually laughing. The way she used to. Her dark hair was up off of her beautiful neck and he felt a stab of envy go straight through his heart. Had Wilson made her laugh? He hated the thought.

Suddenly he knew one thing. He'd be willing to let Josiah Wilson have his beloved if he could make her laugh, could make her come to life again. Trac never could, and it hurt to know it.

Tearing his eyes away, he found some of the men and they began an easy game of horseshoes, which he was able to do as long as he didn't throw all his weight into the pitch. Being unable to do hard work was getting on his nerves. He longed to let Job have his head and ride the range as fast as the animal could carry him.

The entire day was a lesson in human nature. Women looking at their beaus, love-struck and happy to be outdoors after the long winter months inside, and cries of new babies as mothers showed them off, men dressed up in their finest pulling the ties at their necks, and mothers' elated announcement of new betrothals.

Trac found a lone tree stump and sat on it, glad to get away from the fray. He enjoyed the shade of a cottonwood while watching people from a distance.

Janie and Josiah came into view again. This time her small hand was in the crook of his expensive coated arm. He'd had enough for one day. Without a word to anyone he found Job and climbed up, rather stiffly, grunting with pain and headed home.

He hadn't gotten two paces when he heard his name, "Mr. Cordera. You're leaving so soon?"

Trac turned his mount and cuffed his ear. "Ma'am?"

"Miss Laban." He corrected himself when she gave him a long look.

"There, that's better. Now where are you going?"

"Heading home."

"Oh, do stay a bit longer. My father has taken a seat among the elder gentlemen and will be talking the rest of the afternoon. I am out of his sight and wouldn't mind a walk."

Trac smiled, sauntered back and dismounted. He hooked Job's reins to the post got him some water and said, "I shall see that you get your walk." He offered his arm.

Her hand, white with long, slender fingers, took his elbow. "Now what shall we talk about? Politics. Religion. The topics people are so afraid to speak of?" She looked at him square in the eye.

Trac smiled.

"I don't see why people are afraid. We are who we are." She looked up at him, her green eyes sparkling.

"A rising revolutionist?"

"Hardly." She reprimanded him with a look.

She spoke easily of several subjects and then suddenly pinned him with a question. "Mr. Cordera, what do you plan to do with the rest of your life?"

Surprised at the change of topic, he stumbled. "Run my ranch." He stated honestly.

"And?"

"And what?" He was stumped.

"Run your ranch and what?" She repeated. "Surely you plan to have a wife and children."

"Sometime. Not now." He felt a drip of sweat run down the back of his neck.

"And why is that? I hear you're coming up on thirty."

"True enough." He agreed giving him a moment to think. The woman was quick and sure with her words. "I'm in no hurry. Better to marry right than too soon."

"I agree heartily." She pushed a strand of silky brown hair away from her face.

"But life expectancy is short, especially around these parts. Men work themselves to an early grave. Better to marry young enough to enjoy your wife and see your children grown."

"Suppose that's true."

"I've been asked that same question a dozen times."

Trac looked down at her, not understanding her meaning.

"To become betrothed." She fixed it for him.

"I imagine you have." Trac said with a smile.

"You have a nice smile. I've rarely seen you smile." She said smartly. "And what makes you say that." She inquired so sweetly, capturing him with her bright eyes.

"Well, you're intelligent, ladylike, and – beautiful."

"That's all?"

"What do you mean? Those are attributes any man would enjoy, Miss Laban."

"Abilene." She said thoughtfully.

"Abilene." He repeated.

"Well, that's all fine and good, but I want to be someone's companion as well. Someone who will walk beside a man and help him. With real duties, not just smiles and lowered lashes."

"I'm sure you will make the best companion."

She smiled sweetly, "You say the kindest things, Mr. Cordera."

"Trac."

"Trac" she repeated, slipping her hand in his elbow again.

They walked along for awhile in silence then turned to go back and join the others. "Well, I have certainly enjoyed myself, Trac."

"And I."

"Shall we meet at church next Sunday?" She asked in her straightforward manner.

Trac nodded agreeably.

"Then let's part friends and look forward to the future." She inclined her head, snapped open her parasol, and sashayed away, her feminine skirts swaying.

Trac watched her go and admired her for who she was. He intended to meet Miss Laban Sunday next.

Chapter 35

J anie watched from afar, her hand on Josiah's arm, her eyes looking at Trac. So he'd met the beautiful and accomplished Miss Laban. She was the county catch. All the women envied her outspoken wit and intelligence. And she played the pianoforte with a flourish not known or allowed in most homes. Her grandmother had left her a fortune, it was said and her father adored his only daughter. Every man within a hundred miles adored her beauty and wit. Secretly she wished for Trac's happiness, yet stubbornly tried to push her own heart's desires out of the way. It would never be. She'd hated him too long. Or had she?

She felt Josiah pull at her arm insistently. "Come, we need to get the child. It's getting dark and I don't want to have my Phaeton ruined with all the dust the wagons will raise if we leave when everyone else does."

Janie looked at him and sighed. He was so full of himself. So unlike Billy. She berated herself for having allowed this reunion even for today. "By all means. I am fatigued and I'm sure Willa is tired of being carried from hand to hand. I must feed her before we go." She sighed.

"Be quick about it." He said smiling between thin lips.

She hurried to do his bidding, promising herself she'd never go anywhere with Josiah Wilson again. He had no spontaneity at all. But then neither did she these days.

Quickly she found a private place in the woods and sat on a fallen log and fed her child, then hurried to Josiah's carriage. It was easy to find, being the brightest in the long row of gray weathered farm wagons. He was already sitting on the seat tapping the whip.

"Come." He said irritated and let himself down quickly, pushing her up into her seat, smiling, tipping his hat and nodding at passersby who noticed his beautiful conveyance.

He straightened his back and slapped the whip. Janie jerked as they pulled forward. The evening was beautiful but Josiah never noticed or if he did didn't say so. He wasn't interested in conversing when no one else was around, Janie noted.

Willa squirmed and fussed loudly.

"Can't you settle her down? She's ruining the ride."

"She's tired, Josiah. Babies get tired after long days without naps."

"You should have napped her, then." He was cross.

"You insisted I stay on your arm, *for propriety's sake.*" She reminded him.

He said nothing.

When they dismounted, he waited around. "I'll go in and light your way," he said quietly. That was not his usual way. Trac did it but she expected that of him. Josiah never was kind unless he wanted something.

"Thank you. I'll put Willa down."

He made himself busy and in no time Willa had been changed and was snug in her bed and sound asleep in minutes.

"That's a nice sound."

"What?" Janie listened.

"The child sleeping." He said irritated, then caught himself. "Children are a gift from the Lord." He quoted Scripture. "But they can be irritating when a man is courting a woman."

Janie turned from him only to be caught by her wrist and jerked back. "What?" She called out, but found he'd tightened his grip when she tried to pull herself out of his embrace.

"Now, since you've been married, I'm sure you have missed... shall we say evenings in the arms of a man."

His meaning was clear.

"Let go of me Josiah Wilson, or . . .

"Or what? Have you anyone to call?"

She knew she was in trouble. "You unhand me this minute or I'll let Trac know exactly what you're about." She screamed at him.

Her loud voice must have brought him to his senses, for he released her.

"You would do that wouldn't you? And after he killed Billy." He ground out His gaze was pathetic.

"Trac didn't kill Billy." The words came between clenched teeth, fists formed at her side. Billy did a foolish thing and he died. But at least he died doing what he loved." She cried out.

"And where does that leave you? And her" He pointed at Willa.

Janie had no answer.

"It's just as I thought. I have offered for you more than once, even given you a second chance. Since I've gotten the bank presidency I have more choices." He dusted one sleeve then the other in a high-handed manner.

"Then why don't you take them?" She was tired.

"It's you I want Janie. Plain and simple." He was coming at her again and this time his words gentled her fear. "I can care for you. I can give you a house in town. You can associate with the best ladies, have your tea parties and beautiful dresses, while I make a life for us."

Janie backed away but he caught her upper arms and pulled her to him, than landed a kiss on her lips with an intensity that frightened her. She was unable to breathe and tried to wriggle free.

"Oh don't be coy. Every man knows that a woman married before – well shall we say she is hungry for another man?" And he kissed her more urgently. He hands were all over her and she was screaming.

"Do be quiet. You'll wake the child and she'll be screaming."

He finally let go. "Get out of here! Get out of here!" Her rage knew no bounds. All the pent-up feelings of grief, anger, hated, loneliness pounded in her brain.

He backed away at her unladylike shouting. "I'll be back and you will change your mind. You should consider yourself quite lucky to have a bank president for a husband." He sneered and shut the door behind him.

Janie paced and cried, paced and cried. She fell to the floor in a heap. Hurt. Unbelievably alone and disappointed, mostly in herself.

Chapter 36

It was Monday – wash day. Janie had promised to help Louisa beat her carpets, scrub all the bedding, and refill the mattresses with new straw. It was such a beautiful day but the ache in her head from lack of sleep and last evening's row with Josiah had left her upset.

She gathered Willa and when Emmett and Virginia came in the wagon for her, even he commented on her lackluster countenance. He was only teasing, of course, but Janie had no disagreement with his comment.

"I'm awful sorry about Billy." He said.

"I know. It's been almost a year and I'm still . . . well I'm still . . .

"Janie, time will help, his gentle voice and easy manner calmed her heart. "I know Louisa worries when I go off panning for gold but what's a man to do? We can't live life safe in our own cabins and never try anything. Billy loved what he was doing when he died. Does that help at all?" He glanced sideways concerned he may have offended her.

"Yes." She wept now for she had said the very same words just the evening before.

"God has his ways and we don't always understand. The thing is, you can pick up and live again or you can die and go to Billy, having wasted the life God gave you."

"You sound like a preacher." Her voice came out in a half-laugh, half sob. "Maybe I should tell Louisa."

"She'd like a preacher for a husband much better than a gold digger." He agreed wholeheartedly.

"I think you're right about that."

"Mama would like that." Virginia said from her perch in the middle seat.

He slapped the reins, glad for the lighthearted talk.

* * *

The cleaning day went too fast to suit Louisa. The men were all out on the range and Louisa had agreed to wash their bedding along with her own. Trac had stretched extra lengths of rope between trees to accommodate the large number of sheets and blankets. The wind blew graciously.

"Oh Janie, you're here. This batch is ready to rinse and be hung." Louisa swiped a hand across her forehead.

Before long the entire area around the cabin was aflutter, looking as though it were a great ship on the high seas. The women laughed at the scene before them. Multi-colored sails whipped in the wind while Virginia ran between them, under them and all around, her laughter carrying on the wind. She tried not to let a sail touch her. If one did she let out a hair-raising shriek.

Emmett made himself scarce around the cabin preferring to carry water up for the washing than be put to woman's work.

Wes' cooking smelled so good, the ladies went down and begged him to let them sample his stew, promising to send down a batch of apple dumplings to make up for what they ate.

"Wes, you're feeling mighty chipper today." Louisa noticed.

"Yep." He smiled. "Good reason to." He winked at them and left, watching their heads turn awaiting an explanation but receiving none. He left them to their thoughts and went back to work whistling.

The women walked back up the hill to finish their washing wondering when Wes would make good on what the whole church was buzzing about—Mrs. Preston and Wes sitting together.

By evening's end the wind-dried bedding had all been replaced on the dozen or so beds down in the bunkhouse and in the two beds up in the cabin.

Emmett taught Grace how to spoon feed herself at supper "Now maybe you'll leave your ma alone for awhile, he teased and Louisa turned a bright pink.

Janie took herself away from the table feeling like an outsider. "I'm going down to bathe. I'm soaked through with sweat and it's warm this evening. Willa's asleep. Would you mind?"

"Of course not." Louisa's eyes shone with joy these days, happy that her husband was home.

"I'll be back before dark."

"Of course. Go have your bath, Janie...it's been a long, hot day." Then she added, "I shall have a surprise for you when you return."

Janie stopped and turned. A surprise. She hadn't had a surprise from anyone in a very long time. For some reason unknown even to herself tears came rushing up. What could it be? She wondered as she walked to the creek, carrying a borrowed dress from Louisa, a length of cotton to dry with and soap.

Alone now, her thoughts turned to Josiah's harsh treatment of her the evening before. She agonized whether or not to tell Louisa and decided against it. She didn't want to burden her now that she and Emmett were so happy. She'd been so helpless this entire last year, so dependent on everyone else, it was beginning to grate on her nerves. She needed and wanted to be stronger.

Janie spent some time sitting on the banks of the rushing creek. It was nearly dark and she'd not heard voices. Quick like she hung her dress and towel on a low branch where she could reach them then grabbed the rope Emmett had tied to a cottonwood tree, in case the swift current tried to take a body downstream or threatened to drown them. She tied the rope around her waist and tipped her toe in then slowly lowered herself. Gasping at first at the cold rushing water she found her footing, then laid her head back and floated. She washed her hair with the soap and rinsed, feeling wholly refreshed.

Then she saw the shadow of a male figure on the banks. "Who's there?" she shouted, glad she was fully submerged.

"It's me, Trac."

"What're you doing here?" Her teeth chattered.

"I came down to make sure you're all right. The stream is too strong, you shouldn't be here alone."

"Oh is that why you came?"

"Yes." *What was wrong with her now? She was always shouting.*

"Turn your back." She ordered.

"My back is already turned." He ground out. "I didn't come down here to spy on you Janie."

She pulled herself out of the water and dressed quickly, never taking her eye off of him for a moment. Throwing her long soaking hair behind her, without bothering to gather it up, she marched past him, taking the long way around.

"Whoa. I only came to see if you were okay. When Emmett told me you'd come down alone, I . . ."

"Right. I'm sure you came down to protect me. Or maybe you think like every other man around these parts . . . that I'm free for the taking because I've been married." She shouted over her shoulder still in a huff.

Trac caught up with her and grabbed her wrist, pulling her to a stop. She cried out.

He looked down at the small wrist that lay in his big hand, then pushed back her wet sleeves. "What are these bruises from?"

"None of your business. Now unhand me this minute, Trac Cordera." She yelled frantically.

"Why? And let you stomp off in a rage without an explanation? You're staying right here until I hear all, do you understand?" his voice dangerously low. "Now where did you get these bruises." He said slowly.

She laughed, nearing hysterics, trying to wriggle free from his hold but he would not let go.

This time Trac was not letting her get away. He took her shoulders, her wet hair tangling in his hands, and turned her to face him.

She was inches away from the handsome face that haunted her dreams. Hate. Love. Hate. Love.

He waited.

She confessed in an instant.

"Josiah . . . he . . . he." She sobbed against his shoulder.

"He what?" Trac demanded as he pushed her away seeking her eyes. "Did he force you Janie?"

"No, not like that, but, but he wanted to."

"Damn him." Trac let her go and spun, his fists heavy at his side.

She had never heard him swear and it frightened her. Maybe she shouldn't have told him. She stepped back.

"Trac, I shouldn't have told you." She whimpered quietly, her hands wringing at her waist. She was shivering part from fright, part from cold.

The towel lay long forgotten on a branch nearby but she ran for it now and pulled it around her shoulders. Trac turned to see where she had gone and followed her.

"You're freezing." He shrugged out of his leather vest and wrapped it around her. "It's not much. Let's get back to the house."

He started for Louisa's then redirected her without a word and with his hand in hers led her to the bunkhouse and then his office. "The men are asleep." His voice quiet. He lit the gaslight on his desk, and motioned for her to sit.

He reached around and pulled a blanket off his cot and placed it around her shoulders.

"Why didn't you tell me right away?" he said, pain in his voice.

"I can take care of myself."

Trac laughed. "Is that so? Is that what you've been doing all this time, Janie? Taking care of yourself? Is that why you insisted on staying at the ranch? Don't you know woman, that men, strong men need help in this territory? There's not a man around here that can live and work alone out here in these rugged mountains. And you're a woman!" He swing his arm recklessly, nearly toppling the lantern. He set it back from the edge. "What is in your mind to think you could make it out here alone?"

He was so angry, he didn't trust himself to be in her presence one minute more. He turned and left her standing there. "I'll go up and get Willa." He called over his shoulder and kicked up dust all the way back up to the ranch. The foremost thought in his mind right at the moment was sending his fist right into Josiah Wilson's smiling face.

For the next two days he walked around so touchy even his men left him alone.

Chapter 37

B y the end of the week things began to settle back into place.
The summer had arrived in full splendor. Settlers were
making more trips to town for seeds and new gardens were being
set out in hopes of a favorable growing season. Wes had turned up
the rich earth behind the bunkhouse. It was small but he knew how
to use his space to get the most out of it.

Emmett and Louisa were working on their own garden. Now
that Emmett was home it would be large and well-kept. Virginia
walked along behind carefully planting the tiny seedlings. Janie
had stayed with Louisa because Trac had flat-out refused to take
her to her place. He'd told her she'd not be out there alone waiting
for Josiah Wilson to show up. Not even Emmett would listen to
her pleas. He agreed with Trac.

She was burning mad at him now. How did he expect her to
plant her own garden? She was in the way now that Emmett was
back and truth to tell, she wanted nothing more than to pity herself for having to see daily all the many ways Emmett and Louisa
loved each other. She could hardly stand to watch them. Louisa
tried to be discreet but Emmett was always doing sweet little
things and Janie saw every one of them.

She would be going home, if she had to walk.

"Have you got your old stockings on and your old shoes?"
Louisa asked Virginia. "We're going to finish planting today. I've
been looking forward to getting these snap beans in the ground.
According to the Almanac, we're already a week behind, but
better late out than never out, like mama used to say."

Emmett kissed his wife goodbye and joined a few neighbors to help at a barn-raising ten miles down the road. Trac's men could not be spared, so Emmett had offered his services. Louisa also knew he carried a tiny gold nugget to give to the family. They'd lost everything in a fire caused by the eldest son who'd carelessly tipped over a lantern in the house. Emmett hadn't wanted the boy to take all the blame for his family's disaster and hoped to offer the nugget as a start to rebuilding all that they'd lost. Louisa loved him for it.

And Janie's regard for Emmett grew.

By mid-morning the ladies were dusty and dirty. The earth was fairly soft but so very dry. They'd already made several trips to the creek. "We need more water," Louisa announced, wiping her brow.

"I'll go this time." Janie offered and raised herself from the ground holding her aching back. It'll be good to stand."

From underneath her place in the shade, Virginia called, "Ma can I go? Please, I can help."

"Oh Virginia, the creek runs too swiftly darling. Stay with Grace and Willa won't you? Aunt Janie will go."

"Oh Ma, please." The babies are asleep.

Louisa looked up, her bonnet shading her eyes. "Virginia I do believe I detect a bit of sassiness."

"No Ma, I just want to help. I can do chores too." Virginia kicked a rock and a puff of dust flew upward.

Louisa's thought went from a mother's to a woman's heart – back and forth. The child wanted to help. She was the eldest. The woman in her wanted her daughter to be unafraid, to learn hard work, and not be fearful; the mother in her wanted to protect her child from any source of danger.

"All right. But you must stay close to Janie and do what she tells you. Come here." Louisa stood. "On your way find a strong branch that is taller than you. There are plenty on the ground."

Virginia nodded.

"Now place the small bucket on the end of the stick and hold it over the creek and fill it. You are not to get near the banks, do you hear me? They are slippery and not to be trusted."

"Yes, Ma. Hold the stick out over the water. Don't lean or fall in." She repeated.

"That's right. Now remember the cautions I gave you. This is an important lesson." She winked at Janie when she saw Virginia's solemn look.

"Yes Ma."

Virginia ran ahead and Janie sauntered behind her. She would have to find a stick first and that may take awhile. By the time Janie sighted the creek she could see Virginia leaning over the banks, bucket in hand. Alarmed, she began to run. How had the child gotten here so quickly?

Just as she crested the last small hill she watched horrified as Virginia's little body hurdled into the raging waters. Janie spotted the blue gingham dress as it disappeared.

Janie screamed from her gut and ran. Without thinking she slid down the embankment and scanned the water. She spotted the blue dress and then it was gone again. Janie jumped in and tried to swim in the strong current but it was impossible. She held her breath and struggled against the confinements of her clothing but nothing would stop her.

Her last thoughts were of Willa. Reaching and calling, her lungs screaming for air she saw the blue gingham and seized a handful of it. Quickly, she pulled and pulled until finally Virginia was underneath her arm. Her strength wasting away quickly, she grabbed at a branch, missed and tried again.

They were farther downstream now and she could see Virginia's face. Then she was gone, dear God, she saw the breath go out of her. Janie screamed. She couldn't let Virginia die. Moments later she felt strong arms pull her from the water.

Trac had heard the commotion. Louisa had heard Janie's cry of alarm and knew something was wrong. She too ran for the creek. Trac had passed her running. He heard Janie's scream farther down and ran toward it. She was struggling against the branches trying to hold on.

Trac pulled her up and Janie screamed and pointed to the blue gingham. Trac ran and jumped in the fast-moving water.

For three days Virginia lay in a comatose state. The doctor had come from Stonewall and declared her near-drowned. Janie had feared her already gone, but the doc said she was still alive. All they could do was wait for God's hand to bring her back or take her home with Him.

Virginia lay in Emmett's and Louisa's bed in the big room where her parents hovered over her.

Janie begged Trac to take her home but no one would let her leave. Never did she know such depths of sorrow. First Billy and now Virginia.

She woke suddenly from a deep sleep and it occurred to her that Willa would need feeding. She tried to get up from her bed they'd made on the floor. How long had she lain here thinking about herself? She wondered in disgust. Her legs nearly gave out as she saw Louisa's tear-streaked face for the first time in two days.

"I'm so sorry…" She couldn't finish.

"Please don't blame yourself. We must be strong for Virginia." She whispered as she took Janie into her arms.

"I'll get you some tea." Janie pulled away.

"You'll do no such thing." Louisa admonished. "You saved my daughter's life. If you hadn't jumped in and found her . . .

Janie stood in awe. Louisa saw only the good she had done, none of the bad. She'd been asked to watch Virginia and she'd failed. How could Louisa be so forgiving?

"Louisa, may I have Willa? I haven't fed her and I can't remember when—"

"I've fed her." Louisa said quietly as she worked.

Janie found the rocker and collapsed. "You fed her?"

"Of course. You were not well. You swallowed a lot of water, Janie. Trac had to carry you back, don't you remember? You've been asleep all day and night."

Janie put her face in her hands and wept.

Louisa came to her and knelt. "Janie, don't begrudge yourself so. All is in God's hands. We can do nothing but pray." She said softly as she walked to the cupboard, then handed Janie a cup of tea. There's plenty to eat on the stove. You must be starving. Can you manage?"

Janie looked up and nodded. She drank the tea and stood on shaking, weak knees and returned to her bed. She could not eat.

Sometime later the solemn quietness was broken by the familiar squeak of the front door, but Janie did not look up.

Trac knelt beside her pallet. "Janie."

She jumped but didn't have the strength to move.

He called her name again and she felt him tugging at her hands. "Look at me."

"Just go away."

Before she could protest she was being lifted gently into his strong arms.

"Put your arms around my neck, Janie." he commanded tenderly.

She did.

He carried her but she could not look at him. She could feel the wind blowing her hair, then felt herself being rocked. He had carried her onto the front porch and sat holding her in the rocker like a child. She couldn't speak. Couldn't even protest. She was so weak and it had been so long since a man held her.

She was powerless to move and felt his rough hand gently rubbing her back.

"You are so small." He whispered into her hair. "So frail."

Tears began in earnest now and she could not stop them. "Why do you care for me when I have hated you?"

"Because I know you don't hate me. You hate it that Billy died. But you don't hate me."

"I have Trac." Her voice was hoarse. "I hated you so deeply it frightened me sometimes."

"I know, honey. I know. It was misplaced anger. That's all. It took me some time to figure it out, but the Lord has ways of getting to the stubbornest man this side of the Rio Grande."

"Is Virginia going to be okay?" She drew back to see his eyes, where she knew the answer would be.

"One way or the other she will be."

Janie watched as Trac's eyes held hers. "It's time." He said softly as he lifted her chin with his finger. Ever so slowly he leaned closer and paused, his eyes holding hers, then closer, until his lips touched hers in a soft, gentle kiss.

His hand caressed the back of her head as he deepened the kiss. Janie felt herself melt against him as he cradled her closer to his hard chest, her arms going around his neck.

Trac thought he'd never known a sweeter moment. Janie soft in his arms.

Slowly he let her pull away and she buried her face in his neck.

She didn't squirm or try to get away. Trac just held her for long moments until he felt water running down his shirt.

He pushed her chin up for a look. "Janie, are you sorry?" And waited for her answer, heart beating furiously.

When she shook her head, and saw her eyes, he knew.

He pushed her head down to his shoulder and held her close to make sure she knew she was safe in his arms, always would be.

They stayed in the rocker until just dusk. Finally Trac carried her half asleep and put her back on her pallet.

A great weight had been lifted off his shoulders. When he'd seen Janie and Virginia's life hanging by a single branch he'd nearly gone crazy. He headed down to the bunkhouse, wiping tears away, knowing sometimes God has to bring his people close to death to show them how good life is.

And after that kiss, Trac knew there was no turning back.

Chapter 38

On the seventh day Virginia surprised everyone. "Mama can I have water?"

Emmett and Louisa jumped awake at their daughter's bedside. "Of all things, you want water?" Louisa cried joyfully and ran for a cup.

Once Virginia was all right, Janie wanted to go home. "I'll take you." Emmett said happy to be busy.

"Trac will take me." Janie said quietly as she lifted Willa and walked to Virginia's room.

"Thank you Miss Janie." She heard the soft scratchy voice from across the room.

"I'm just so glad you're here." Janie set Willa on the bed and instantly Virginia's eyes lit up.

"I'm sorry if I scared you."

"You did scare me, but you mustn't be sorry. God helped us both. Trac pulled us out together."

"He did?" Virginia's eyes grew huge in her thin face.

"Yes. You and I must both thank him."

"I will." Virginia said softly and Janie could see she'd fallen back to sleep.

"Thank you Lord, for sparing Virginia's life and mine...and for Trac." She whispered and stood, Willa smiling in her arms. "It's time to go home." She said to her daughter.

Emmett rode down to the bunkhouse and asked for Trac. "He's gone to Janie's place." Wes informed him.

Emmett brought the wagon back up and waited while Janie gathered her things and said her goodbyes.

She was so tired of running from one house to the other, hoping to find comfort. It was spring and she wanted to scrub floors, sew curtains and take Willa for rides in her little wagon. And...Trac was at her ranch.

"I'm ready." She kissed Louisa, and Virginia and Grace and pulled herself up then took Willa from Louisa's arms. She thanked her friend with her eyes and waved as they pulled away.

She pondered the last few days and wondered if she'd been in her right mind. Had Trac kissed her? Had she let him? Would he still want her after all the hatred she'd carried for him all those months?

Emmett pulled the wagon up to her house. It looked so forlorn and quiet sitting there the only movement was the wind blowing the newly budded trees.

"Trac must be out in the fields. Don't look like anyone's here." He noted.

Janie smiled and felt her heart drop a peg. "Thank you Emmett...for bringing us back. I'll get my things and you can get home."

He hopped down and helped her unload. Janie could see he was anxious to go. "Thanks again." She said, her hand covering her eyes at the sun and watched as the dust blew up and he disappeared.

Willa was put down for a nap and it was time to clean. A bucket of water and some lye soap would do. She scrubbed the floors, found matches tucked between the wooden floor slats and remembered the days when she grieved. Tears fell into the bucket and on the floor. Then sobs tore through her. "Billy Cordera, you left me. You left me."

Janie could not remember how much time passed as she scrubbed and cried out over and over. She would not be here alone, thinking about Trac if Billy hadn't left her. She felt guilt crawl up and take residence in her mind. It raged against her. Against Trac. Against the world. She cried herself out and realized she'd come to the doorway, finishing the room.

Janie grabbed the bucket of dirty water and poured it out on the new flowers that were just beginning to pop out of the ground. It was a comfort. The floor was clean, her soul cleansed as well, and the flowers watered. She pulled in a deep, shaky breath, dropped the bucket on the porch and grabbed the broom and began to sweep furiously.

Trac found her like that.

He wondered if she had reverted back. The way she was going at it reminded him of the day he found her that same way right after Billy died.

Job slowed at his touch and he waited out near the pines to watch her from afar. That woman had stolen his heart the first time he'd laid eyes on her and he had forced his feelings out of his heart for so long, he could hardly believe it was true. He had kissed her. Held her.

If anything happened now, he knew it would break him. Slowly, he dismounted and meandered up the path leading to the house watching her as he went. He stopped dead in his tracks when he saw her finish sweeping the steps and look out over the land, hand on her hip, a smile on her face.

He continued to walk. Faster. Would she feel the same as before?

As he neared, he called her name.

She turned, put her hands above her eyes and he saw the sweetest thing. A smile rested on her face.

He hurried up, eyes locked on hers.

She set the broom aside and arms at her side, waited.

In seconds he had her in his arms, twirling her around. "Stop. Stop. You're making me dizzy." She laughed.

He stopped, but kept her near. She was different now. Not the carefree young girl he once knew. Her face showed another Janie. One more acquainted with the grief of this world. One who knew darkness at its deepest level.

If it took forever, he was going to put the light back into her eyes. It would be different but he was going to spend the rest of his life making sure of it.

The wind blew the wisps of her hair and Trac could not wait one more minute. He had to know for sure. He leaned down to kiss her again and held her close. He removed his hat and walked arm in arm to the porch where she informed him they would sit. The floor was still wet and she wasn't about to tramp dust on that clean floor.

Trac didn't mind one bit.

Chapter 39

T rac preferred eating alone tonight.
He and Janie had talked for two hours that night and he'd walked around in a daze for three days chomping and chewing on every word she spoke. She made him promise to wait several months to see if they felt the same. He'd feel the same. But he knew she needed time.

If he had to wait for a year he would, but he knew one thing. He'd have to stay away from her as much as possible. So he was sitting in his office, drawing out plans to build a new ranch house. Times were hard and women were best off if they had a man especially if they had a child to raise. People understood the hardships of living on the wild Montana plains. Trac knew the folks would be all right with him and Janie marrying.

He thought about Billy, too. He would have ordered him to, if he could talk down from heaven. Trac smiled at that thought.

The men had taken dinner at the long trestle table built for them. He'd carried his plate into his office.

"Boss" Wes called through the door.

Trac nearly fell out of his chair. "Yeah."

"Can I have a word with you?" Wes entered. "Anything wrong, boss? You look a little blue behind the gills."

"No, I just tipped my plate." He uttered from underneath his desk.

"You okay? Your back ain't givin' you trouble is it?

"No. I've worked on the kinks finally. Just tired, that's all." He took a seat.

"Boss, I been needin' to tell you something and I need a bit of advice."

Trac waited, throwing his booted feet on the desk easily.

Wes tipped his chair back against the wall and added his booted feet to the small desk. His chair creaked loudly.

"I been thinking on asking a woman to be married up with me. But I don't rightly know exactly how to go about it."

"Oh?" Trac made him suffer.

Wes looked from under his hat and continued. "Yep, I guess you know it's Mrs. Preston I'm speakin' about."

"I do."

"Well, you see, it's like this. It's been so long, I ain't sure about what a good society woman expects from an old worn out cowboy like me. Now I got me a pretty good sized bankroll, since I been single and all, but I'm not real certain a lady like Mrs. Preston would be happy living out here on the ranch. Providin' I built a real fine house, do you think a lady like her would stay out here in Montana? I know fer a fact she's been wantin' to go back east." He cast a look at his boss.

"Did you ask her?"

"No. You think I'm crazy? Seein' as she's a lady and all, I knew I wasn't up to the score. That's why I'm askin' you 'bout it." Wes scratched his head.

"Well, the way I see it, since I have never been married before, I don't see how I can be of any help to you, Wes."

"Well, then, I guess you ain't no good to me." He took his feet off the desk and let his chair legs fall to the floor and stood.

"Hold on." Trac motioned for him to sit. "I do have one idea."

"And that is?"

"If you want you can buy out that Northwest corner. There's ten acres there that would get you a good start. And if you want to add a little more later…"

"No man. Don't want nothing but a small patch. I'm too old and rickety to do more'n plant a garden and get your cookin' done. I'm plumb tired. No more cattle rustling, no more farming. 'Sides that I'll have more riding back and forth from my place to yours if I go and do that."

"Suit yourself." Trac grinned.

Wes reached for his tobacco pouch and then put it back.

"You quit?" Trac asked smiling.

"Yep. She don't allow no kissin' if I been a'chewin'. I quit for nigh unto two months now, just habit, I guess. Anyways, back to the reason I bothered you a'tall. How does a man gettin' to be my age ask a pretty society woman to be married up with the likes o'me?"

Wes' face was so serious Trac had trouble keeping a straight face.

"Naw, probably she's just bein' nice and ain't got no reason to up and marry a dude rancher like me." He said sorrowfully, shaking his head.

He was so distressed, Trac could hardly control himself.

"Ask her."

"Just like that. Come right out like that? Ain't it supposed to be sweet-like?"

"Does she know how you feel about her? Have you told her?"

"Yeah." He winced and turned blood-red. "I couldn't help myself."

"Did she say anything back?"

Wes started squirming. He took his hat off and twirled it in his hands. "This is awful embarrassing, boss."

"Well?"

"Yeah . . . yeah, she did at that."

"Well, then what're you waiting for? What's she gotta do, mash you over the head? You're not getting any younger Wes."

"You're right about that, boss." He reached for his tobacco pouch and put it back again. "You think it's okay to march on over there and just say it outright?"

"I certainly do. A woman as beautiful as Mrs. Preston might just have other gentleman callers."

Wes was on his feet now. "You heard o'any?" He frowned. "I'm headin' out right now." He sputtered, punching his hat on.

"Wes...She's at Janies."

"She's at Janie's you say?"

"Yep, better get going. Those summer church picnics have a way of settin' women up with all kinds of romantic notions, if you know what I mean."

"You don't think she'd up and marry some dandy from the east do ya?" Wes worried himself.

Before Trac could answer, Wes headed for the door.

"Wes, don't you think you should change your shirt?"

"Oh yeah." He looked down.

In less than ten minutes, he was back in his best trousers, a clean shirt, and Trac noticed his boots were shined clean of dust. He settled a brand new gray Stetson on his newly washed head and with one last look, walked out the door.

Trac got up from his chair and shut the door after him. "Poor man." He muttered and knew exactly how he felt.

Chapter 40

Mid July brought hot weather. Trac worked extra hours. Two of his hands took jobs in the next county and it doubled his work. He took to riding drag, which meant he had to round up the lost cattle and ate enough dust to last him a lifetime. His men offered to take the low position. He'd refused. "I was riding drag a long time before my pa would allow me up to flank rider position. I earned my way up. Besides I can handle the difficult animals, the whole stubborn lot of them." What he really meant was he had to stay away from home as much as possible.

Emmett and Louisa and the girls had settled into their routine again and for the twentieth time he missed Billy riding drag with him, it hurt to think about it.

"You sure take a lot more baths down at the creek." Dan had kidded him bringing him to the present.

"I go down to swallow some of that good clean water. wash out some of that dust I eat all day long." Trac laughed.

"What's up with Wes? He's been burning the vittles, even forgot to cook breakfast yesterday." Cash called out loudly several nights later.

Trac smiled and against his better judgment, spoke. "Woman's got his brain all tangled up."

The men needed no other incentive. Some of them groaned, some whistled, some laughed, already thinking of how they could make some new jokes with Wes.

Wes came walking out from the kitchen, his apron hanging loose. "Now why'd you go and tell 'em that?" He stared at Trac.

"Aw, we all knew, Wes. Just givin' you a little medicine for your trouble," Riley called out.

"You all know?"

"We've been knowin' for some time now, so don't look like you spilt the beans." Tan sided with Riley.

Wes turned and stomped back to the kitchen.

The men heard the rock and rack of pots and pans. "Little loud in there ain't ya?" Riley called out.

The hooting and hollering made Trac laugh in spite of it all. Sure as the sun came up in the East and cattle birthed in the spring, a woman could upset a man's life just by walking past him.

Trac was glad Emmett was home to help with Janie's place, woodcutting and water carrying for the animals, which allowed him more time in the bunkhouse taking care of bookwork when he wasn't driving the herds.

He noticed, too, that the fine Mrs. Preston had visited Louisa twice this summer already. And that Wes was pretty scarce around those particular times.

The county was all in a'twirl. There was to be a wedding come September. Wes would be joined in matrimony to Mrs. Sara Preston. Just last Sunday the announcement had been reported at church and by now even Trac's men knew.

There was already a flurry of activity and the wedding was weeks off. After church the ceremony would be held and dinner on the grounds afterward. The women were scurrying around making new dresses, sewing new bonnets and planning for their daughters to use the occasion to meet eligible young men.

Wes took so much teasing from that day on, Trac asked the men to lay off for awhile. "Give the man time to think. He may change his mind and then where would all of you be?"

The men considered that their meals might go away, or they'd get some awful cook and took it upon themselves to keep their mouths shut, with an occasional remark making it to Wes' ears.

As the days passed Wes was getting more and more nervous. "Where'd I put those biscuits?" Trac heard him growling from the kitchen.

Trac walked quietly to the cook's area and watched as Wes pulled open the cook stove doors one by one.

"They're sitting on top. Right there." Trac pointed.

"Well, why didn't you say so?" Wes muttered.

Trac shook his head. "Wes, you need tomorrow off?"

"Nope. Don't let me off boss. I'll just be ridin' around in circles. I'm so nervous now I'd forget where I was. Best I stay here."

"Hey I've got a big load of steers to ride back to the range, over 500 head. You want to go along?"

Wes stopped long enough to process the thought and jumped in with both feet. "Sure, you bet, boss. When do we leave?"

"Two days out. Got a wire yesterday saying they're on the way."

"Count me in. Who'll take over the cooking?"

"The men."

Wes processed that quick. "You're jesting right? They don't know a thing about putting together a meal."

"Well, seems to me they ought to appreciate the fact you've been slaving over that stove for nigh unto fifteen years and as much as they like your cooking, I'm thinking they'll like it a whole lot better when you come back."

"Only be about ten days. Think they can manage?"

"Well, I'll be durned. Never thought o'that. But I'm thinking you might be right about that." Wes smiled and laughed out loud. "I'll be durned."

Two days later the load arrived. Trac took Wes and he rode with him at the rear. "Eatin' dust again." Wes coughed. "Ain't done this in a long while. Feels mighty good to be in the saddle again. Little stiff come evening, but I figure this'll be the end of the trail for me."

"Why? Just because you're getting hitched up." Trac, tired and dusty and hungry tossed Wes a look.

"Got me some land to clear and a house to build." His cook shot back. "Beings you have most of the money I've saved up all these years." He added.

"True enough." He laughed. Wes had paid him cash for the ten acres.

"So you ain't buyin' that I'm broke solid."

"Nope." Trac kicked his spurs into Job and rounded up a couple of strays.

Chapter 41

Trac had spent the last month and a half getting the fences up and the cattle driven back here and branded. He'd added a good amount to his herd now that he could take care of his own ranch. And Emmett had proved to be a better rancher than he'd expected. He'd always hated ranch work he said, but Louisa said he hadn't minded too much lately. Trac hoped, for his sister's sake that Emmett would take up ranching.

And there was news! His little sister, Molly was due back from Boston. Older sister Margaret had kept her for an entire year and Louisa had missed her. Trac wondered how much she had grown, since she left at fourteen and was past fifteen by now. Louisa's heart was bursting with joy. First her husband and now Molly would be there in time for the wedding. It seemed nothing could be more perfect.

Trac rarely saw Janie, busyness kept them from being in the same place at the same time. When he did see Janie, they had little time to be alone.

Trac enjoyed the peace he felt in his heart. He'd had time to grieve Billy. And he missed his cousin as much as he missed his mother and dad. They all lay up on the hill in the same small fenced area under a stand of weeping willows. He stood next to the graves under the weepy limbed trees and stared at the cross he'd made. It was weather-worn already and he could hardly believe it had been more than a year. So much had happened in that short span of time. Miss Olivia Kipper, from the General Store had married a young land surveyor, and last he heard she was headed West to California. Wes was about to become a husband, with a built-in granddaughter.

"Trac." Emmett slowed his horse. "We were wondering where you were. The girls sent me for you. Molly's arrived on the train. Since the girls are still putting their heads together for this wedding, you and I are appointed to get Molly and bring her back as quick as the wagon will carry her." He laughed

Glad for the interruption, he hopped up on his faithful mount and headed down to the bunkhouse. "I'll change. Been a busy morning." He explained and noted that Emmett followed at a slower pace, his hand shielding his eyes from the sun, looking out over the blue Big Belt mountains in the distance. The man was seeing what Trac always knew was there. A wild beautiful Montana if you could abide the winters.

Within the hour they were traipsing along the well-worn trail. "Louisa's missed Molly." Emmett said quietly. "She's hoping Margaret hasn't changed your little sister's mind about going back to Boston. She's had so few letters from her."

Trac nodded, but said nothing. He knew Margaret to be strong-willed and very superior in mind and good looks. And would likely already have Molly signed up for special girls boarding school. Truth be told Trac learned that a body was born with something deep and innate inside of them. He could no more head East than he could give up seeing these mountains every day of his life. He understood. If Molly loved it here she'd stay, if she didn't she'd head back East.

The men pulled their wagon to the side and waited for the train to come down the track, then went into the station and caught up on the latest news, the grain prices, and whatever else the men there wanted to talk about.

Within an hour, Molly stepped off the train and Trac didn't recognize her. He thought her to be a handsome young women… which she was…not the little sister he sent off over a year ago.

"Trac, Emmett." You both look the same." Tears dimmed the brown eyes.

"Come on. There's a wedding in a couple of days and Louisa and the girls are anxious to see you." Emmett grabbed her carpetbag.

"I have one trunk. It's rather large, I'm afraid"

"We'll get it." Trac followed his sister, her dress obviously of East Coast quality. Several young men thought so too. He gave them warning looks and decided that she was probably going to head back to Boston as soon as she could arrange it.

Emmett followed and the two men muscled the huge trunk onto the wagon. "What do you have in here?" Trac groaned, his back reminding him of the last time he ended up in bed for two weeks.

Gifts from Margaret…and me." She said sweetly. "For all of you."

Trac winked and helped her up, then he took one side, Emmett the other and they were off.

When the wagon rattled to the ranch house, Trac and Emmett waited for the outrush that came pouring out the door. Much talking, and looking over her new dress and soon the ladies were at the table catching up over tea and biscuits.

Janie was absent. And he missed her. But she had refused to break into the family reunion. He would fix that forever as soon as she gave him the word.

Chapter 42

"Yes, you need tomorrow off, it being two days before the nuptials?"

"Nope, don't let me off, boss. I'll just be ridin' around in circles. I'm so nervous now I'd forget where I was. Best I stay here."

"Suit yourself." Trac snapped on his chaps, settled the Stetson on his head, and headed out for a day's round up.

Saturday night baths were had all around.

Sunday morning, Wes' wedding day dawned bright and clear. Trac could hear the women talking. Emmett had gone early for Janie, Willa, and Mrs. Preston. They were all up at Louisa's. Emmett sauntered down and knocked at Trac's door. "You'd think the President of this United States was coming by, the way they are fussing over all the details. The wedding dress had a speck of dust on the hem and they clucked like chickens with a fox in the henhouse.

Trac laughed. "Best you stick around here until the last hour and then we'll load up and be off."

"Wes down here?"

"Haven't seem him for awhile, come to think of it." Trac bent his head around the doorframe to have a look in the kitchen.

"I'm headed back up. They might need me." Emmett announced and left.

"Good luck." Trac called and set out to find Wes.

"Excuse me." Trac walked through the back door and found Wes staring out at the landscape.

"Wes?"

"Yeah, boss."

"Everything okay? You holding up?"

"Yeah." He stuffed his hands in his pockets and took them out again. He was shiny clean.

"You clean up nice, cowboy." Trac tried not to show his surprise. Wes was a good looking man. His baby blues would stop any women dead in her tracks and with him in his wedding duds, he cut a fine figure.

"This'll be over in a while and you and the new Mrs. Clancy can be off to Helena on your wedding trip."

"Don't talk about it." He muttered.

"What?"

"You know."

"Guess, I don't."

"I ain't been alone with a woman in twenty years, Trac."

Trac kicked at the stones beneath his boots. For once in his life he didn't know what to say. Moments of silence stood between them like those rock buttes out there. They stared at the purple mountains in the distance for a long time.

"Loving a woman's a lot like loving your land, Wes." Trac started. "You see her, she's beautiful, but you don't know her good points or bad points until you've been with her for awhile. You love the good things, dislike the bad things, but you never move. It's home."

"Yeah. Things are sorta like that aren't they boss?"

"Make her a home, love her like you love your land and she'll stay and be your woman." Trac squinted at the sun.

"You're a good man, son."

Trac felt his heart squeeze up.

"How come you ain't got a woman?"

Trac laughed.

"You blind son?"

Trac gave him a look.

"Janie's your woman. You know it though right?"

"That I do, Wes."

"How come you ain't asked for her then? That Wilson chap nearly claimed her right under your nose."

"I know." Trac grumped. "She pretty much blamed me for Billy's death.

"I know that." Wes sounded disgusted. "But you ain't gonna let her get away with that are ya? Set her straight onct and for all. That's what I'd do. Even if I had to carry her off."

"And do you think you would have carried off Mrs. Preston if she'd refused you?" Trac shot back.

"I mighta at that." He said. "Yep, if I'd had to I would have." He decided.

"Think Janie would let me carry her off?"

"I'd be asking Janie if I were you." He let Trac think about that a minute. "You know her mother is worried about her. And well, I don't want Mrs. Preston to be worried none."

"I'll take care of Janie." Trac said. In Wes' current condition he wasn't about to tell him about their plans. Besides Janie made him promise to give her time.

"See to it that you do boss." Wes said in fatherly manner. "It's getting' to be time." He checked his pocket watch, then snapped it shut. "Mrs. Preston would be nigh unto calling the weddin' off if I'm a minute late."

"Let's go. You riding alone Wes?"

"Yep, got to do me some thinking and time to say a prayer or two afore I get there."

"I've got some thinking and praying to do too." Trac admitted. "See you there."

Trac shut and latched the door at the bunkhouse and walked up to the cabin. Janie would be there. His heart beat quicker at the thought. He had seen her only in passing these last few weeks.

The house was noisy even from a distance. Emmett was sitting on the porch rocker looking a bit rundown. Trac knocked and started to walk in. "Wouldn't go in there if I were you." Emmett said easily.

Suddenly the door slammed shut in his face and he heard feminine screams from inside.

Trac joined Emmett in the other rocker.

"It's time we get on the road. We can't be late with the bride." Trac yelled to the women a few minutes later.

"I tried. They won't come out until they're darn good and ready."

Fifteen minutes later Virginia opened the door and stepped out. "My but you look like a fine lady from Boston." Trac smiled down at her. Emmett smiled as his eldest daughter stood before him to show her pa her new pink dress and Trac thought he saw a single tear roll down his face.

"Mama's coming with Grace next. Wait until you see Mama, Papa,"

Louisa stepped out with Grace. "Indeed three ladies straight from the fancy streets of Boston and all with the same dress. How do you suppose that happened?" Emmett asked in mock surprise.

"Papa, you know Mama sewed the dresses. Janie helped too."

Mrs. Preston came out in an old gray dress and Trac's eyebrows raised high on his forehead. "Don't be thinking this is my wedding attire Tracson Cordera." She sputtered. "I absolutely refuse to put on my beautiful gown and have it ruined before I get to the church."

"Suit yourself, Mrs. Preston." Trac clapped his hat on.

"Has Mr. Clancy left for the church?" She inquired sweetly.

"A long time ago."

"Then we must get going. I abhor lateness!"

Emmett raised up and then sat back down when Mrs. Preston said, "Oh not yet, we've got to get Willa dressed. Janie's almost through but she was so busy with everyone else, Willa's still waiting."

Trac ventured inside calling out that he was coming in and was everyone decent? "I'll dress Willa, if you'll tell me what she's supposed to wear." He called out to the ladies in the bedroom behind closed doors.

Janie exited carrying Willa and her dress. "Put these on her, would you Trac? It took all morning to finish Mother's dress."

Trac stared. Before him stood a bundle of pink perfection. Janie's brown eyes looked back at him. "You look beautiful." He managed, jerking off his hat and twisting it in his hands, round and round.

"Thank you." She dropped her eyes and handed Willa to him and then her clothes. "Her stockings and satin shoes are on the table."

Trac took the baby, never taking his eyes off Janie. Even when the door shut he still envisioned her soft eyes and that pink dress.

Coming to himself, he sat Willa on the table after spreading a blanket and dressed the wiggling baby girl in the same dress as the other gals. "You'll be pretty as your mother someday, Miss Cordera" he teased and lifted the child into his arms. Then he wrestled with the little feet trying to get those fancy shoes on.

Janie came out.

"I like your hair." Trac said after a lengthy pause. He tried not to stare, but she looked so much like the Janie he'd seen as the young girl he'd first met.

"Thank you. I decided to change it last minute."

She picked up two bundles and he carried Willa out to the waiting wagons and handed her to Virginia. Grace was with her father. Both wagons, his and Emmett's had been fitted out with new hay, and an overabundance of quilts, with fabric scraps flying in all directions. The remnants were even twisted in the wagon wheels.

"I've never seen such a to-do as this one." Mrs. Preston murmured as she took her place next to Trac. He waited for her to tuck her dress in and helped Janie get into the back with Willa. He winked at the two of them and saw Janie's face color.

Church proceeded as usual except for the fact that it was full to overflowing with parishioners. The wooden benches creaked with the weight of the people. Afterward, there was a time for visiting while the ladies prepared the church for the highlight of the summer ... a wedding.

Little girls were sent flying to pick all the white field flowers they could gather where they were arranged at the front of the church. Ladies brought bows they had been making all month and tied them to the end of the pews. Once everything was set in place, the wedding attendees were called in with organ music. Reverend Dunham filed in last and took his place up front.

The best and finest of Stonewall were sitting inside those walls. Trac and Janie stood up as witnesses which placed him directly in line with her. He took full advantage, smiling at her every now and again when she looked up. His eyes never left hers as the vows were repeated.

"Will you take this man . . . this woman. In sickness . . . and heath."

In his heart he was saying them to Janie. He'd never loved anyone else.

After the nuptials were said the wedding group went outdoors to sing, eat and have a game or two. Trac lost sight of Janie...there were so many pink dresses. He was sipping lemonade under the cottonwoods, when he felt more than saw someone near. "Miss Laban." He greeted the beautiful young woman and removed his hat.

"Abilene."

"Abilene." He repeated and moved to give her access to the shadier part of the ground.

"So when is the next wedding?"

Trac looked at her. "Next wedding?"

"Yours."

"Oh, I doubt . . ."

Miss Laban interrupted him, "It doesn't take a genius to see that you love Janie Cordera." She said easily. Trac turned to face her, his face flushed. He readjusted his hat once, then again and found he could not utter a word.

"Why are you so surprised?" She laughed lightly. "The most handsome man in this county, not to mention you own the biggest share of land available in the county. Why every gal this side of the Rockies would do well by you."

"You speak openly, Miss Laban." He settled his eyes on some children playing stick games. When his dry mouth began to work again, "Is it that obvious." He squinted at the sun and put his hat back on.

"It is, but don't worry. You don't seem the type to rush into anything. Just seems to me she's been a widow long enough."

"Well..." he didn't know what else to say.

"I'm going to seek out a very handsome Mr. Lawrence, my fiancé now and let you seek out your lady." She winked slyly and moved away gracefully.

Trac was taken aback. "Women. You just never know when they're gonna hit you right square between the eyes having never even raised their fist." He muttered to himself and looked through the crowd for Janie.

He found her all right. Talking to Josiah Wilson. And she wasn't smiling. In fact Josiah was pulling on her arm and she was trying to free herself.

Trac picked up a handful of dirt, rubbed his hands together, threw it down and stalked through the crowd, his purpose clear in his mind. Janie never saw him coming and for that he was glad. His movement became more cat-like and before Josiah Wilson knew it he lay flat on his back in the dust and in his expensive duds with blood running down his neck staining his new white collar.

"What?" He sat up sputtering and stood trying to look dignified. "What'd you go and do that for?" He rubbed his jaw.

"Don't you ever let me hear you've laid a hand on her again, Wilson. You understand?" he ground out.

"Janie." Trac grabbed her hand.

"Don't worry, she isn't worth it . . ." he started to say more but reneged when Trac Cordera turned back, his black eyes burning with desire to punch him again.

"Oh dear," Janie said aloud as she was running alongside Trac faster than she could carry herself. "Slow down."

"Sorry, Janie. I saw him handling you and I lost my senses."

"I'm glad. He was trying to make me walk with him alone."

Trac stopped and turned, his face red again.

"Lets try to have a good time. It's mother's wedding day." She spoke softly.

"You're right and I'm a fool to have lost my temper." He slapped his hat against his thigh.

"I'm glad you did." She said sweetly and put her hand in his elbow as Trac slowed his step.

He looked down at Janie's hand resting on his arm.

"Let's go find Willa." She needs to be with us. "He looked above the crowd. "There she is." He pointed and headed out.

Trac reached down and pulled the chubby nine-month old into his arms. She squealed with delight and he threw her up in the air a couple of times. "She likes that." He laughed.

"Yes, she likes that."

A line formed with the bride and groom at the head. Goodbyes, good wishes and blessings were sent from all around and the party began to break up. Chores awaited the men.

Emmett settled his family in their wagon and since Mrs. Preston was now Mrs. Clancy, Trac had his wagon all to himself. "Janie, you and Willa are riding with me."

She came gladly and the three of them rode home beneath a full moon, the music of the summer night frogs keeping them company. Willa lay sleeping on her mother's lap.

Trac pulled the wagon up near the porch, helped Janie down then went in ahead to light the gas lamp. Janie placed the baby in her cradle and slipped off her shoes.

"Janie." Trac knew his heart was beating overtime as his arms went around her. He tossed his Stetson in the direction of the corner. She wrapped her arms around his waist and he reveled in the feel of her next to him.

His voice rumbled above her ear. "It's taken so long." He whispered and drew back.

As he told her he loved her with his eyes, he slowly bent down to kiss the woman he loved more than life itself. To make sure she knew it, he took her face in his hands and kissed her again.

When he heard her sigh, he pulled her fully into his arms and held her close.

"Trac," she whispered, "I'm so sorry."

He released her and took a step back. Then you don't . . ." he couldn't say the words. He felt his heart turn to stone. "It's all right you don't have to say it. I understand." He reached for his hat and turned when he felt her hand on his arm.

"I'm sorry for all the pain I put you through. I couldn't think of anything except how my heart was broken. You lost your best friend…your childhood friend…" she paused tears wetting her eyes. "I am sorry." She couldn't speak another word.

He nodded, punched on his Stetson and turned to leave.

"If you walk out that door, Tracson Gage Cordera, you'll break my heart again."

Had he heard right? What did she mean by that exactly. He had to know. He turned and walked up to her.

"Look Janie. There isn't anything that will change the fact that you and I lost Billy. But we are still in this world and as long as we are, I'm going to do whatever I can to see that you and Willa are taken care of. Is that clear?" He knew he sounded gruff.

"I see." She said quietly. "I need you Trac. Is *that* clear?"

Trac stared at her, bending slightly to read her eyes and found what he was looking for. He pulled in a breath, thinking he almost walked out because he misunderstood her words.

"I love you…" she whispered then stepped back at his frown. "What's wrong?"

"I intended to utter those words first." Trac paused then smiled.

"Then why didn't you?" She had her hands on her hips and he wanted to catch her up and twirl her around. Which, when he thought about it was exactly what he should do. So he did.

"Put me down." She laughed.

He did, but he didn't let her go. "It's good to hear you laugh, Janie."

Suddenly her laughter turned to tears and Trac held her closer and let her cry on his shoulder.

"What changed your mind?" He asked gently.

"When you jumped in to get Louisa and me I knew you could never do anything to hurt Billy. But I was so bitter, blaming you, that I couldn't see it. Not until that day. And then I knew."

"Knew what?" Trac wanted to hear her say it.

"I saw your look, felt your gentleness, and knew that you had been grieving too, yet you put aside your grief to make sure Willa and I survived. And you honored Billy by taking care of his ranch, his widow and his child."

Trac could stand no more of this.

"Janie, I know you want to wait…

She stopped him with two fingers over his lips. "How could I not love you? I'm just sorry it took so long to forgive you."

"I'm not sorry Janie. There were some beautiful times, even when things weren't exactly perfect. It took all those things to make us who we are now."

Suddenly he was on one knee before her. "Please don't Trac!" She pleaded.

"Don't what?"

"Don't kneel. I'm the one who should be kneeling." She cried as she pulled at him to stand.

"Come on down here with me then Janie and we'll seal this pact on our knees. Before the Lord."

She did.

"Will you Janie Cordera, do me the honor of becoming my wife?"

"Oh yes . . ." Tears streamed down her face.

Trac wiped them away with his thumbs.

He brought her up with his hand in hers and for long minutes kissed her soundly, making sure he branded her forever with his love. Leaving the cabin that night was one of the hardest things he'd done in a long time.

She heard the wagon creak and groan as it moved away. Her heart told her to run to him. This time she listened and obeyed.

"Trac. Trac. Please take me into your arms once more." She sobbed, running alongside the wagon. He pulled hard on the reins, threw them down and jumped to the ground and ran back, swinging her round and round.

"I just had to be sure." She said softly. "I just had to be sure."

"You can be sure Janie." He stated firmly. "Marry me a month from today?"

"Yes. Yes. I'll need that time to make a dress."

"Whoa doggies." She heard him roar as he drove away, his hat circling in the air.

Chapter 43

The next morning Trac was pounding on her door. He'd paced out under the moonlit skies for most of the night. He prayed. He laughed. He prayed again. As soon as the sun rose, he drank a cup of coffee, the worst he'd had in a long time, since Wes was gone, and picked an armful of wild flowers.

"Trac." Janie whispered and he took her into his arms. "I've been waiting all night to do this again." He laughed as he lifted her off her feet.

"You are not in possession of a sound mind." She squealed and woke Willa.

"You're right about that."

"I've never seen you so … so "

"So in love with a woman?" He finished for her.

Shyly she looked down and smiled. Her bare feet stuck out from beneath her gown and robe. "Put me down, Tracson." She hurried away to dress.

Trac spent the day with her, Monday or no. He'd left explicit instructions with Riley at sunrise that the men were to continue their assigned duties and he would be gone for the entire day, not to be disturbed.

"Something wrong boss?" Riley had asked seriously.

"Yep. I'm afraid there is Riley."

Riley waited with concern written all over his face.

"I'm in love with Janie." He whooped and woke the entire bunkhouse. Within minutes his men knew.

"That's not news!" One of the guys shouted out.

"We were just waiting for you to see it yourself." Riley explained, glad the news was good.

The men came over and clapped him on the shoulder. "You knew?" He looked at Cash. "And you?" He stared at Dan. "All of you knew?"

The men nodded one by one.

He wandered out of the bunkhouse and straight over to Janie's. "You're here for the whole day?"

"Yep. What're you going to do with me?" Trac tossed his hat on the nail.

"First of all I'll make breakfast. It won't be as good as Wes' though."

"Won't matter." Trac picked up Willa.

"Then, since it's Monday we're going to wash. Then we'll weed the garden, and then water it. And then..."

"Whoa woman. Who's the boss around here?"

"At my house . . . me."

"He encircled her waist with his big hands and gave her a twirl. "You can be boss, just don't ever forget I love you."

"How could I Trac? How could I ever forget?" her eyes filled with tears.

"Hey. No more crying. You've cried enough this year." He sobered.

"I want you to know I promised Billy I'd take care of you and Willa." He whispered, holding her close.

Trac had made a pledge and she knew he would keep it. Janie wiped her eyes and smiled. Today she would stop crying tears of pain. Forgiveness was freeing. She was alive again.

THE END

Epilogue

Exactly one month later on a mid-October day Janie and Trac were married at the little church in Stonewall. Thunder rumbled in the distance while little Willa clapped her tiny hands unafraid.

As soon as the ceremony was finished the women grabbed their food and placed it on the front pews as Trac and the men carried the two tables inside. The hoopla continued inside as everyone shook the rain off and celebrated. Trac's eyes surveyed the crowd until he found Janie. They exchanged looks and her longing eyes drew him to her like a calf to its mother.

"I still can't believe all this." He waved his Stetson in a semi-circle.

"Well, believe it Trac, because you are a husband and a father all in one fell swoop. You have your work cut out for you."

"Work? You call this work?" He drew her close. "You're beautiful in that dress." He growled in her ear.

"Fall harvest will be here soon, sir. Your mind best be on your chores."

"My mind is thinking about how Billy and I planned a new hacienda for his bride. I'm going to build it for you both."

"What?" Janie pulled back, "But..."

"We'll build it back a ways from the ranch house so that when Willa grows up she can live in it while we have our own hacienda at the back of the property right next to the Red Canyon River, just like he planned. He wanted you to hear the rumbling of the water over the rocks when you went to sleep every night."

"I never knew that." She whispered.

"Of course you didn't. It was our secret, Janie. That's why Billy was riding that stallion and I upped the ante...so he could get the gold to build your hacienda."

Janie started crying all over again. On her wedding day.

Trac grabbed her arm and swung her in tune to the violins and banjos playing off to the side. "We're going to dance."

She smiled as she let Trac lead her.

Then one year later to the day, little William Gage Cordera was born. But this time Louisa attended Janie. Trac was setting up the walls of the hacienda and didn't make it back in time. Will was a strong boy and did not seem to possess the inclination to wait for his father.

Two more girls followed promptly behind William. Mr. and Mrs. Clancy were frequent visitors to the new family. And Wes turned out to be the *best* grandfather.

LaVergne, TN USA
06 February 2011
215464LV00003B/2/P